MENLO SCHOOL

founded 1915

MENLO COLLEGE

Gift of

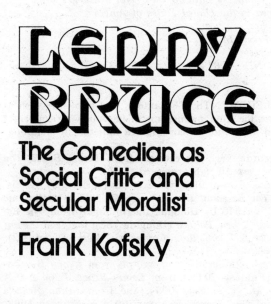

LENNY BRUCE

The Comedian as Social Critic and Secular Moralist

Frank Kofsky

MONAD PRESS, NEW YORK
DISTRIBUTED BY
PATHFINDER PRESS, INC.,
NEW YORK

ACKNOWLEDGMENTS: The author and publisher wish to acknowledge the kind permission of the following copyright holders and agents to use copyrighted material in this book:

Bizarre Records, Inc., for excerpts from *Lenny Bruce: The Berkeley Concert.* All rights reserved.
Douglas Book Corporation, for excerpts reprinted by permission from *The Essential Lenny Bruce,* © 1967 by Ballantine Books and © 1970 by Douglas International; from *The Essential Lenny Bruce: Politics* (Douglas 788); and from *Lenny Bruce: To Is A Preposition, Come Is A Verb* (Douglas 2). All rights reserved.
Fantasy/Prestige/Milestone, for excerpts from *Lenny Bruce— American* (Fantasy 7011); from *Lenny Bruce: I Am Not A Nut, Elect Me!* (Fantasy 7007); and from *Lenny Bruce's Interviews of Our Times* (Fantasy 7001); © Fantasy 1962. All rights reserved.
Phil Spector Productions, for excerpts from *Lenny Bruce Is Out Again* (Philles 4010). All rights reserved.
Trinita, Inc., for excerpts from *Lenny Bruce: The Midnight Concert* (UAS 6794). All rights reserved.
Marvin Worth, for excerpts from *How to Talk Dirty and Influence People,* © 1963, 1964, 1965, 1966 by HMH Publishing Co., Inc. All rights reserved.

TO CHUCK B~~ROW~~N
Musician, composer, mentor,
peerless companion and friend,
and another lover of the art
of Lenny Bruce

contents

Ppeface

The commercial success of *Lenny,* a late 1971 New York theater production dealing with the life, death, times, and work of Lenny Bruce, demonstrated the existence of a large (and probably expanding) market for Brucian memorabilia. Thus the deluge of new books, articles, and recordings on that controversial figure, with a movie or two about Lenny waiting in the wings.

Although this book, too, appears after the initial run of *Lenny,* it pleases me immensely that it was not conceived as an attempt to join the necrophilian stampede to cash in on the memory of Bruce. On the contrary, the idea for such a work originated in the winter of 1970-71 — before *Lenny,* that is — out of my correspondence with Leon Litwack. A professor of history at the University of California at Berkeley, Litwack, like myself, had been a follower of Lenny Bruce for over a decade. In 1970-71, as a member of the Program Committee of the American Historical Association (AHA) — the oldest society of professional historians in the United States — he persuaded his fellow committee members that a special session devoted to Lenny Bruce at the 1971 meeting of the Association would help fill the gap in the Association's coverage of contemporary cultural history, an area which seemingly it has often preferred to neglect (perhaps on the assumption that it would go away).

With the support of the Program Committee behind him, Litwack set out to recruit participants for a session on Lenny Bruce. Although he asked a number of academic historians active in the field of cultural history — all of

9

them more prominent than myself, incidentally — I was the only one to accept. It is out of Professor Litwack's initial request for a paper on Bruce that the present volume has grown.

Since Bruce's ambivalences make up a large part of the subject of this book, especially of the second part, I suppose there is a certain justice in the fact that the book itself took the shape it did as a result of my own ambivalences — specifically, about how Bruce could best be presented to an academic audience. Naturally, I was delighted that the AHA was at last going to give overdue recognition to Bruce and the cultural phenomena he represents (my choice of tenses is deliberate); and of course I could not help being flattered that Professor Litwack, who had read my earliest review of Bruce in 1961 and was sufficiently taken with it to remember my name almost ten years later, wanted to include me in a scholarly program devoted to discussing Bruce's work and its significance.

On the other hand, the assignment to prepare a paper on Bruce — actually, by the time I had agreed to participate, it developed that mine was going to be *the* paper at the Bruce session — became increasingly troubling and intimidating the more I pondered it. Ordinarily, if one were setting out to analyze the work of a person for a session at the AHA, one could operate under the assumption that most of those who would hear the paper would be familiar in a general way with the life and career of that person. Not so with Lenny Bruce, however. Professor Litwack had told me that the historians who had declined to participate in the AHA's Bruce session gave as their reason lack of knowledge of the subject! If these savants, whom I would have thought to be the profession's most *au courant*, with-it, and culturally hip, as it were, didn't know much about Bruce, then the average AHA member could barely be expected to have heard Bruce's name. Or so I reasoned.

In that case, perhaps something like "An Introduction to the Thought of Lenny Bruce" was called for as my contribution. Yet there were drawbacks to that approach, too. For one thing, there were certain to be at least a few historians who were acquainted with Bruce's work; surely they would expect more than just a simple exposure to his wit, satire, and morality. Placed in that situation myself, I know I should have wanted to hear about why Bruce was of great enough importance to justify a prestigious special session dealing with him. And, since this was going to be a paper read initially to an audience comprised mainly of historians, shouldn't there also be some attempt made to understand how Bruce's analysis of society was rooted in and grew out of the circumstances of the man's life, how his private concerns had been broadened and reshaped in his public performances?

It was my ambivalence over the proper way to present Bruce at the 1971 AHA meeting that caused me to drag my feet in preparing a paper on him. Eventually, as my deadline drew nearer, I saw I was not going to be able to resolve the ambivalence about what aspects of Bruce I should discuss, and decided to abandon even trying to resolve it. Instead, hoping that I could still somehow miraculously keep the paper at manageable length, I decided to combine approaches: I would write both an introduction to Bruce *and* what I hoped would be a more probing investigation of the sources of his thought.

The result of that decision is, in all essentials, the essay on Bruce you are presently holding in your hand. It is probably not necessary to say that my hope of keeping such an ambitious project to a length short enough to be read at a session of the AHA, even a special session given over solely to it, was nothing more than an exercise in self-delusion on the grand scale. This, combined with the fact that our session was forced to start late and end early and that media representatives were much in evidence throughout, meant that the session was probably more chaotic and less immediately productive than either Professor Litwack (who chaired it) or I had anticipated; we were both disappointed on that score. (In fairness to Professor Litwack, whose kindness in asking me to write on Lenny Bruce touched me deeply, I must add the caution that neither he nor anyone else should be saddled with any responsibility for the theses on Bruce that I advance in this essay; that is properly the author's due alone.)

Nonetheless, I have deliberately chosen to allow those opening remarks directed at the historical profession to stand unchanged; it would be dishonoring the memory of Lenny Bruce to do otherwise, in my opinion. For in the wildly unlikely event that Bruce himself had ever been asked to address such a gathering of historical scholars, it is a safe presumption that he would not have hesitated to remind his hearers — in the context of a barbarous and genocidal U. S. war against the peoples of Southeast Asia — of the obloquy and condemnation heaped upon German academicians after World War II for their having given passive or active support to Adolf Hitler's Nazi regime in order to safeguard their own lives and professional careers. Such a reminder, with its implied comparison, would be supremely appropriate for the members of the American Historical Association. To their incalculable disgrace, this elite among professional historians has shown itself no more willing collectively to oppose the U. S. government's callous and methodical slaughter of entire civilian populations in Southeast Asia than their German counterparts were willing to oppose the bloodthirsty policies of Hitler. At no time, for instance, have the Association's members ever adopted so much as a principled denunciation of the actions of the U. S. government in Vietnam, Laos, and Cambodia — thus indicating, to my mind, their tacit acquiescence in those actions — though to have done so would not have brought, as was the case in Nazi Germany, severe reprisals onto the heads of either the leaders or the members of the AHA.

In light of this fact, it seemed to me that any program designed to elucidate the life and work of Lenny Bruce — if it were to do more than provide an occasion for the members of a scholarly association to congratulate themselves smugly on their singular sophistication, broadmindedness, and liberality — would at least have to attempt to be faithful to the spirit of Bruce himself. This meant that, even at the risk of appearing ungracious, it would have been highly irresponsible of me had I not utilized this opportunity, as I presume Bruce would have done in an infinitely more skillful and palatable manner, to reiterate to the historical profession what ought to be its obligation to serve the highest values of humanity against the powers of reaction, obfuscation, mass murder, and wanton destruction. For Lenny believed, as we shall see, that if there were truly any four-letter words that could be considered "obscene," they were such terms as *kill, maim, hurt,* and the like. What is more, it was his contention — one still to be understood by the scholars, alas — that moral principles should be a guide to *action,* not merely a set of precepts held abstractly. Consequently, he was unsparingly critical of those who claimed to be acting in the Judeo-Christian tradition but at the same time failed to uphold the unambiguous condemnation of all killing found, for example, in the Ten Commandments.

While this latter point may have particular relevance for academicians, especially historians, in the U.S., its relevance is by no means limited to them. Granted that not all of my readers will be historians, is it any the less imperative to underline the connection that ought to exist between one's morality and one's actions? That, in any event, was the view of Lenny Bruce, who had the novel conviction that morality meant something more than conventionally pious sentiments, sanctimoniously intoned with eyes rolled heavenward. It meant, in his lexicon, active beliefs on which one could — and should — base one's life. The incongruity of the American Historical Association's sponsoring a program on Lenny Bruce while still cravenly refusing to rise to a condemnation of the U.S. war on Southeast Asia is just the sort of flagrant contradiction of humanitarian rhetoric combined with cynical expediency that Lenny would have found an irresistible target for his telling barbs. If dwelling on this contradiction helps fix his idea of a unity of theory (morality) and practice in our consciousness, then clearly there is ample justification for allowing my remarks directed at the members of the AHA to remain herein.

Much to my dismay, none of the provocative criticisms of the historical profession in the U.S. implicitly posed by even the most cursory examination of the life and thought of Lenny Bruce received serious discussion at the special session on Bruce at the 1971 AHA meeting. Indeed, the fatuity of most of the commentary contributed immeasurably to my feeling that the session had been a virtually futile gesture. At the same time, however, I must admit that one of the commentators, Margot Hentoff, raised a point (albeit a narrow one) regarding my essay that I think merits an attempted rejoinder.

Beginning with the entirely correct observation that we have no documentary record of what Lenny Bruce was thinking around the time of the Rosenberg trial and the heyday of the late Senator Joseph McCarthy, Ms. Hentoff went on to infer that Bruce's better-known views in the late 1950s and early 1960s — the consistent opposition to capital punishment, e.g. — were simply those that were fashionable among Jewish young people (Bruce was then in his mid-thirties) of the period. While it is possible to agree with Ms. Hentoff's premise, one must dissent completely from her conclusion. There can be no argument with the proposition that Lenny Bruce's ideas during the earliest years of the cold war are not precisely known to us. On the other hand, if we are to accept Ms. Hentoff's thesis, we would have to believe not only that Lenny was sucked into the maelstrom of the national cold war psychosis, which is difficult to accept but possible; we would further have to accept the notion that, subsequently, Lenny misrepresented his previous convictions, presumably in order to save face. Yet anyone who has studied Bruce's written and spoken words attentively knows that the man went out of his way to be as completely and painfully candid about himself with his audience as was humanly possible. It strains our credulity past the breaking point to impute this sort of behavior to Bruce, since it is wholly at variance with everything else that we know, intellectually and intuitively, about him.

More than that, Ms. Hentoff's syllogism rests on defective logic. Since Bruce's views as of, say, 1960, are those of the conventional young Jewish liberal on such issues as capital punishment, she reasons, then perhaps his views of 1950 were correspondingly those of the Jewish liberal of that day. Ah, yes — but you see, the *essence* of Lenny Bruce is that he was not a conventional liberal, that he transcended liberal "wisdom" at every opportunity. To be sure, there are occasions, as is the case with his opposition to capital punishment, where his view and the liberal position coincided. What this means is not that Lenny was espousing the cliches of liberal dogma, but that the liberals had come around to *his* point of view. You can find in his recordings (most done in the very early 1960s) and in his autobiography, *How to Talk Dirty and Influence People* (serialized in *Playboy* starting in 1963), passages in which he manifests his concern with what most of us, since we have become alerted, now think of as: Black Power; prison reform and the rights of convicts; the plight of Native American peoples at the hands of whites; repressive anti-homosexual laws; the right to abortion; education about venereal disease; and so on. Naturally, Lenny did not hang these capital-letter labels on his topics. Given his milieu and his ostensible profession of comedian, that would have been both silly and unproductive, not to mention wholly out of character. What is important is that where Lenny's sentiments did coincide with liberal ideas, you can be certain that Lenny generally got there first.

And, of course, the corollary is that Lenny was continually forging beyond beliefs that most liberals were able to endorse, transcending all the sacred liberal cliches in the process. The touchstone, as I see it, is Lenny's adamant refusal to be taken in by bullshit U. S. cold war ideology. He wouldn't buy air time for Radio Free Europe to sell "freedom." He thought Cuba, not the U. S. Navy, had the better claim to Guantanamo Bay. He wouldn't take the hot-lead enema to save the Important Military Secrets. And he said — ultimate heresy! — that if communism cooked for you, solid. But all of these attitudes put him absolutely out of step with liberals — 1950s liberals, 1960s liberals, or whatever. They may, like Lenny, have had an aversion to capital punishment in the case of Caryl Chessman; but more likely than not they were, as Lenny was emphatically not, one hundred and ten percent behind Kennedy-style liberalism in the Bay of Pigs fiasco and the made-in-U. S.A. "Cuban missile crisis." Here is where Lenny's views were so greatly removed from conventional liberal platitudes that at times it must have hurt.

So Margot Hentoff's speculation that Lenny Bruce may
have swung with the times from a 1950s hard-line position
to a 1960s knee-jerk cold war Jewish liberal one, while
superficially plausible, is in actuality extremely far-fetched.
It misses what is most crucial about Bruce—namely, that
he continually and consistently saw through and rejected
ideology, especially (but not exclusively) cold war ideology, once he became aware of it. He always put the demands of being human above the demands of *any* conventional ideology. Thus he went considerably past the tame
limits of liberal thought in repudiating out of hand the
waging of the cold war—well over a decade, at that,
before the U. S. Establishment got around to conceding the
existence of the People's Republic of China—which is why
his views in the 1960s would have been anathema to most
liberals, had they ever learned of them. To see Bruce as
parroting whatever happens to be the currently faddish
slogans therefore, is fundamentally to misunderstand this
already tragically misunderstood figure.

For if one maintains that Lenny Bruce's concern, con-
sciously or otherwise, was primarily to align himself with
ideas and causes that were favored by political liberals,
even those of his own age, then surely it must also be conceded that he took a most curious way of going about it.
In truth, however, such opportunism was wholly foreign
to Lenny Bruce—in the 1950s, no doubt, as much as in
the 1960s. (For that matter, was advocating clemency for
the Rosenbergs, or even mentioning their names, *ever*
such an instant route to popularity, even in the 1960s?)
Indeed, had he been of a more opportunist bent, conceivably he would have better mastered the art of self-preser-
vation. Hence the fact that an essay such as this can
now be written is testimony, after a fashion, to Lenny's
inability even to attempt to tack with the prevailing winds.
Lenny ended by giving his life to establish this point. There
is no historical interpretation in the world powerful enough
to destroy the force of *that.*

There are a number of people whose assistance was in-
valuable to me in the course of completing this essay.

Mary Jean Brackmann and Dianne Kennedy worked patiently and tirelessly up to the last minute to insure that the manuscript was typed and duplicated in time for the 1971 American Historical Association meeting in December. Ms. Mann—Molly to her friends—was an equally excellent typist and, more importantly, a peerless transcriber of Lenny Bruce from tapes and records. Without Leon Litwack's invitation to read a paper at the 1971 AHA meeting, I doubt that I would have had sufficient incentive to embark on such a project as this. The members of my late-afternoon class in Education and Ethnicity in the Twentieth Century during the fall of 1971 were good-humored enough to allow me to try out many of my ideas about Bruce in that setting. My thanks, inadequate as they may be, go to all of them.

FRANK KOFSKY

March 1973

PART I

The Phenomenon

. . . Bruce's performance [is] in the great tradition of social satire to be found in the works of such . . . authors as Aristophanes [and] Jonathan Swift.

Attorney Albert M. Bendich[1]

The . . . people who really dig Lenny Bruce are the people who are doing the same thing Bruce did—cutting loose, turning on, turning away, trying to turn America around.

John Cohen, in his Epilogue to
The Essential Lenny Bruce[2]

. . . The primary fact about Bruce . . . is that he is extremely funny.

Kenneth Tynan, from the Foreword to
Lenny Bruce's *How to Talk Dirty and
Influence People: An Autobiography*[3]

# of Lenny Bruce

Before trying to understand Lenny Bruce the man, it is necessary to say something about Lenny Bruce the phenomenon.

One aspect of that phenomenon is the fact that Lenny was, as I will illustrate, literally hounded to his death. Another aspect of that same phenomenon is that, as I write, there are two theatrical productions in New York—a city whose courts once judged Bruce's public performances to be "obscene"—devoted to his life, work, and death. The malicious irony in this, of course, would probably have appealed strongly to Lenny, who could always be relied upon to find a touch of bizarre humor in virtually anything, his own predicament emphatically included. Thus he could greet his "obscenity" conviction in New York with the laconic remark:

What does it mean for a man to be found obscene in New York? This is the most sophisticated city in the country. This is where they play Genet's *The Balcony* [which itself was only a mild forerunner of what was to come—no pun intended]. If anyone is the first person to be found obscene in New York, he must feel utterly depraved. [4]

19

One could laugh at this only because one knew, as did Lenny himself, that he was just the opposite of "utterly depraved."

If anything, in fact, Lenny Bruce was a highly moral man who refused to deviate from his strict code even when it would have been enormously to his advantage to do so. For instance, one of the reasons he was busted so often, Lenny believed, was because he rebuffed and then publicly exposed an attempt at extortion made for the trial judge by a prominent Philadelphia attorney at the time of Bruce's first "narcotics" arrest in that city (1961):

> I was approached by an attorney who has since died —
> he was one of the biggest lawyers in the state — he could
> have gotten Ray Charles a driver's license.
> "How do you do, son, could I talk to you? I don't
> know if you've heard of me, but I understand you had
> a little beef today . . ."
> And he promised to quash the whole thing for
> $10,000. [5]

Interestingly enough, as with all but one of his arrests (and he claimed innocence in that one, too), Lenny was vindicated in this case. Indeed, doubly, albeit posthumously, so: the grand jury refused to issue an indictment against Lenny, and the judge who had solicited a bribe through the attorney was subsequently removed from the bench and denied reinstatement by the U. S. District Court. [6] Lenny could most likely have avoided further judicial harassment by paying the bribe or, at the very least, keeping quiet on the subject. It was his outrage at seeing the law so perverted — together with a touching, if rather naive, faith in the U.S. system of "justice" — that led him to speak out. Even though in the long run — when Lenny was long in the sod, that is — his position was upheld, in the short run, during his lifetime, he suffered, and suffered grievously, for the secular sin of acting honestly upon his convictions.

Another instance of Lenny's sacrificing material advantage for the sake of conscience occurred in his 1963 "narcotics" trial in Los Angeles, when he attempted (unsuccess-

fully) to avoid being compelled to swear on the Bible,
thus prejudicing the members of the jury against him. 7
Here again, Lenny was betrayed by his faith in the power
of truth and reason as weapons, and his corollary tendency to underestimate the extent of official venality and
incompetence. One of the so-called doctors who testified
with unshakable certainty that Lenny was a heroin addict,
was later discovered (by a private investigator that Bruce
employed after his conviction) to have been fired as super-
intendent of a Tennessee hospital for "mismanagement"—
such mismanagement extending to the completely illegal
castration of a patient without that patient's consent! Likewise, the star prosecution witness against Lenny—who in
retrospect appears to have been trying to divert suspicion
from himself—was a police officer who was subsequently
"arrested, tried, convicted and sentenced to jail for having
smuggled drugs into the U. S."8 Of such threads was the
fabric of justice, or what passed for justice when it came
to Lenny Bruce, woven. A momentarily disillusioned Lenny
Bruce himself put it more succinctly: "The halls of justice.
That's the only place you see the justice, . . . in the halls."9

These lurid tales of arrests, trials, and convictions, with
all of their fantastic and improbable convolutions (perhaps less fantastic and more probable, however, than
complacent academicians might wish to believe) are part
of what I have called Lenny Bruce the phenomenon.
Equally so, it is only reasonable (and accurate) to ob-
serve, is the presentation of a paper on Bruce before such
a group of historical scholars. Alive, can anyone seriously
argue that Lenny Bruce's scathing tongue would have
been allowed to address this Association? One may be
permitted one's doubts. What, after all, could he possibly
have said to a body of professional historians who, in
their collective wisdom, were unable to arrive at a condemnation of the immoral and inherently genocidal U. S. aggression in Vietnam? Knowing Lenny's penchant for speaking truth to power, even at his own expense, it isn't at all
inappropriate to suggest that he might have found it fitting
to recite his paraphrase of a Thomas Merton poem, in
which he took on the *persona* of Adolf Eichmann to make
his point:

My defense: I was a soldier. I saw the end of a con-
scientious day's effort. I saw all of the work that I
did. I watched through the portholes. I saw every Jew
burned and turned into soap. Do you people think
yourselves better because you burned your enemies at
long distance . . . without ever seeing what you had done
to them?[10]

Or perhaps he would have been content to use a couple
of lines from his "Religion, Inc." routine: "'Thou shalt
not kill' means just that—it doesn't mean, 'Amend., section A,' it means, 'Stop war!'"[11] And what, one wonders,
would be the response of the historians to *that?*

At bottom, the various aspects of Lenny Bruce the phenomenon are dialectically interconnected: those who loathed
and detested him, as well as those who joined forces to
prosecute him even though they thought him innocent,
had the same reasons for their reaction as those who became the man's devoted followers. Both groups saw in
Lenny someone who was making a wholesale assault,
as opposed to a piecemeal reformist modification, on the
status quo.

To be sure, it is possible to object—and correctly so—
that Bruce did not explicitly espouse revolutionary doc-
trines, that he at times quixotically defended the legal system and even capitalism in the U.S.; the latter he mistakenly equated with business competition rather than
oligopoly.[12] This is quite true, but it is also beside the
point. The sum total of all Bruce's statements on behalf
of the existing social order and its institutions never added
up to anything more than a collection of offhand comments entirely marginal to the major thrust of his work;
they could be eliminated entirely without altering that
work in any significant respect, for they represent a kind
of momentary lapse in the main line of Lenny's thought.
Given Lenny's background (for instance, his unsystem-
atic self-education), his milieu, his temperament (essentially akin to that of the jazz musician, as I will discuss
below), his quasi-improvisatory mode of performance,
and the like, such lapses can readily be both understood
and overlooked.[13]

Lapses or no lapses, the overwhelming bulk of Lenny's humor was directed against those frozen orthodoxies and sacred cows that together comprise what C. Wright Mills — whose views, incidentally, strike me as being enormously close to Bruce's, especially on matters of public morality [14] — christened the "conventional wisdom." For it is precisely the unthinking acceptance of the conventional wisdom, with its biases toward complacency, conformity, cynical amorality, and political apathy, that enables the status quo to be maintained for the most part without recourse to naked force: better dead than red; [15] you can't fight city hall; niggers are all right as long as they stay in their place; [16] honest portrayals of sex or the natural functions are dirty and tend to corrupt, but to witness violence to other human beings is clean and ennobling, especially for children; [17] God is on our side; [18] religious leaders have no business meddling in things they don't understand (such as racism, war, poverty, prison conditions), but should confine their work to leading prayers and fund-raising; [19] there is nothing wrong with a society in which Dean Martin-type entertainers — or corporation executives, for that matter — are paid more in a single week than most teachers earn in a year, [20] or in which people are forced to scavenge for food from garbage cans and live ten to a room while next to them stands a cathedral that cost millions to erect and now remains unoccupied twenty-three hours a day; [21] political leaders are invariably competent, highly moral and, of course, never lie, and therefore are to be believed and obeyed implicitly; [22] smoking marijuana is physically harmful and leads inevitably to heroin addiction, whereas drinking or taking prescribed stimulants and depressants are just harmless and perfectly legal practices that can be given up at any time; [23] the purpose of sending a person to prison is to provide humane rehabilitation rather than punishment; [24] and so on. At one time or another, Lenny Bruce tackled all of these shibboleths with his art.

Moreover — and this is what most likely caused Bruce to be perceived as a threat to the status quo — unlike the intellectuals and academicians, he did not voice his sometimes outraged views merely in the relatively secure isolation of the campus, in the learned journals read by mere handfuls, or in the elite theaters and small art-movie houses. In such places a certain amount of dissent is tolerated, protected, perhaps even cultivated, provided only that it never reach a mass audience or become effectual. Bruce, on the other hand, arrived at an innovation that was, for its time, genuinely revolutionary: he would synthesize the vocation of nightclub comedian with the point of view of a radical social critic. In this way, Lenny was able to reach far greater numbers — and, no less crucial, reach them at a visceral level where his words demanded to be taken seriously — than the intellectual radicals were ever able to do. This, alas, was probably the key to his undoing. Had he been content to write his satirical scenarios in, say, *Partisan Review* or the *New York Review,* he probably would be alive — and wholly obscure — today. As in the case of Malcolm X — with whom, incidentally, he shared a number of interesting parallels, as I will bring out below — Bruce was compelled to pay a heavy price for the privilege of communicating his ideas to an ever growing and ever more committed audience.

If it was Bruce's mass appeal that set him apart from other social critics, it was his radical stance that distinguished him from run-of-the-mill supper club comedians, however gifted. Unlike these performers, Lenny never restricted his wit to safe, socially accepted but essentially trivial topics. On the contrary, what he sought to do, as I have already indicated, was to subject all of society's conventional beliefs to the merciless glare of rational thought. Implicitly, his contention was that no proposition ought to be immune from such scrutiny, whether the case for immunity was made on the basis of sacred status or its secular equivalent, "national security."

It is possible, though probably not ascertainable, that Lenny's probing of society's leading institutions and ideologies became increasingly more radical than he had originally intended, as the pace of harassment by the police, the courts, and the other guardians of the status quo was stepped up. What is not at all open to question, however, is that his biting satire revealed a profoundly moral passion from the very outset. This was apparent in virtually every "bit," as Bruce called the component pieces of a performance,[25] even with something so traditional for the nightclub or vaudeville comedian as impersonations of the famous. Bruce was not only unwilling to recapitulate the typical repertoire of the stand-up comic in the usual manner, but he had a certain amount of disdain for those performers who did.[26] Hence his approach even to something as hackneyed as impersonations, as done in his early bit, "The Tribunal," served to restore freshness to the impersonations and transformed them into the vehicle for a strong comment on the absurdity of existing social priorities:

> I feel some guilt of the fact that my salary exceeds twenty-fold schoolteachers' in states like Oklahoma — they get thirty-two hundred dollars a year, which is a *disgrace,* schoolteachers' salary. Take Zsa Zsa Gabor, who gets *fifty thousand dollars a week* in Las Vegas; and schoolteachers' *top* salary is six thousand dollars a year. This is really sick, to me. That's the kind of sick material that I wish *Time* would have written about [in its treatment of Bruce and so-called sick humor]. I'm not that much of a moralist. If I were, I would be donating my salary, then, to schoolteachers! I admit that. If the man came to me and said, "Well, we're going to levy a tax and we're gonna raise schoolteachers' salary to seven hundred and fifty dollars a week," I would approve of it and pay the tax like *that.* 'Cause I realize it's an insurance factor. If schoolteachers get that kind of money, then the education system will change immediately. I'm a hustler: as long as they give, I'll grab.
>
> But I know that someday there's going to be a tribunal. We'll all have to answer, I'm sure of that. I'm just waiting for the day. I'm saving some money to give back: "I know I was stealing. I didn't mean to take it — they gave it to me." We'll all have to answer; they'll line us up. The guy will be in the black shrouds, all the performers.
>
> *Tribunal judge:* Awright, line 'em up, all the offenders there. State their names and their salaries. The

sentences will then be meted out. The first offender, what is your name, there?

First offender: Frankie Laine.

Judge: How much do you make a week, Mr. Laine?

Laine: Ten, twelve thousand dollars a week.

Judge: It's remarkable!! What do you do to earn from ten to twelve thousand dollars a week?

Laine [*sings*]: "To spend one . . ."

Judge: Burn his wig. Break his legs, thirty years in jail. Get them up here, the next one. What is your name?

Second offender: Sophie Tucker.

Judge: And how much do you make a week, Miss Tucker?

Tucker: Twenty to thirty thousand dollars a week.

Judge: What do you do to earn twenty to thirty thousand dollars a week?

Tucker: I'm the last of the red hot . . .

Judge: Burn her Jewish records and jellies, and the crepe gowns with the sweat under the arms. Get rid of her! Get them up here, the next one — the one that's worshipping the bronze god of Frank Sinatra. What is your name?

Third offender: Sammy Davis, Jr.

Judge: And how much do you make a week, Mr. Junior?

Davis: Twenty, sometimes thirty thousand dollars a week.

Judge: What do you do to earn from twenty to thirty thousand dollars a week?

Davis [*imitating Jerry Lewis*]: Hey, Dean, I gotta ba — [*sings*] "That old black . . ."

Judge: Take away his Jewish star and stocking cap, . . . and the religious statue of Elizabeth Taylor. Thirty years in Biloxi. [27]

In his autobiography *How To Talk Dirty and Influence People*, Bruce remarks that his "approach to humor" lay in "distinguishing between the *moral* differences of words and their connotations" (emphasis in original) — that is, distinguishing the difference between the literal denotation of a word, what it actually says, and what it is used to connote in practice.[28] Frequently, in order to render his subjects with complete verisimilitude — and Bruce was too much the perfectionist to be satisfied with anything less — he had to have recourse to words or phrases that conventionally were considered "obscene." In the course of relating his experiences on the Steve Allen television program, Bruce sought to explain his reasoning on this point:

> I don't make any bones about the fact that sometimes I'm irreverent and sometimes I allow myself — this is a rationalization — the same poetic license as Tennessee Williams, or Shakespeare. In other words, I'll never use four-letter words for *shock* value, for a laugh; but if it *fits* the character, then I want to swing with it and say it.[29]

Nonetheless, audiences continued to be shocked by his straightforward usage of earthy colloquialisms, and Lenny found that he had to address himself to this problem repeatedly in order to minimize the alienation of his audience from him. (Perennially the moral preceptor, Bruce naturally hoped that he could win over hostile members of the audience rather than lose them completely — certain reviewers to the contrary notwithstanding.) Whether or not he was familiar with the writings of Wilhelm Reich — which was by no means inconceivable, since Lenny read both omnivorously and eclectically — he ultimately came to share Reich's view that the authoritarian repression of the natural sexual curiosity of the infant and the child laid the basis for various irrational and repressive ideologies subsequently held in adult life, particularly (but not exclusively) those that emphasized the "dirtiness" of all that pertained to sex, bodily functions, etc.[30] In an effort to undermine the hold of such ideologies on his audiences, and in line with his interest in "distinguishing between the *moral* differences of words and their connotations," he would expound to his listeners:

> I want to help you if you have a dirty word problem. There are none . . . — and I'll spell it out logically to

you. Here is a toilet. Specifically — that's what we're
concerned with, specifics — if I can tell you a dirty toilet
joke, we must have a dirty toilet. That's what we're
talking about — a toilet. If we take this toilet and boil
it, . . . and it's *clean*-clean, I could never tell you
specifically a dirty toilet joke about this toilet. I can
tell you a dirty toilet joke about the toilet in the Mil-
ner Hotel, but this toilet's a clean toilet now. Obscenity
is a human manifestation. This toilet has no central
nervous system, no level of consciousness. It is not
aware — it is a dumb toilet. It cannot be obscene —
it's impossible. If it could be obscene, it could be
cranky. It could be a communist toilet, a traitorous
toilet. It can do none of these things; it's a dopey
toilet, Jim. So nobody can ever offend you by telling
you a dirty toilet story. They can offend you from
the area that it is trite — you have heard it many, many
times.

Now all of us have had a bad early toilet training.
That's why we are hung up with it. All of us, at the
same time, got two zingers. One for the police department, and one for the toilet:

"Awright, he made a kaka, call a policeman. O. K.
Are you going to do that anymore? O. K. Uh, tell
the policeman he doesn't have to come up now."

We all got the policeman-policeman-policeman. And
we got a few psychotic parents who took it and rubbed
it in our face. And those people, for the most, if you
search it out, are censors. [31]

Predictably, however, this straightforward, rationalist
position on dirty words and dirty toilets did not negate
Establishment opposition to Bruce — not especially sur-
prising, inasmuch as the Establishment itself, as Reich
observed, has traditionally relied heavily on authoritarian
and irrational ideologies (e.g., "Yore President knows
best") as a means of ruling while maintaining social
stability unimpaired. The opposition continued unabated,
as Bruce discovered to his chagrin when he was first
arrested for obscenity in supposedly liberal San Francisco
in 1961. The pretext for Bruce's arrest was a bit in which,

characteristically, he was attempting to distinguish between the literal meaning of the word "cocksucker" and its use as a pejorative term to denigrate male homosexuals: [32]

> The first gig I ever worked up here was a place called Anne's 440, which was across the street [from the Jazz Workshop in San Francisco]. And I got a call, and the guy says, "There's a place in San Francisco, . . . but, uh, they've changed the policy."
>
> "Well, what's the policy?"
>
> "Well, I'm not there any more, that's the main thing."
>
> "Well, what kind of show is it man?"
>
> "Well, you know . . ."
>
> "Well, no I don't know, man—like it sounds [like] kind of a weird show."
>
> "Well, it's not a show—they're a bunch of *cocksuckers*, that's all. A damn fag show."
>
> "Oh. Well that is a pretty bizarre show, uh, I don't know what I could do in that kind of a show."
>
> "Well, no, it's—we want you to change all that."
>
> "Well, uh, that's a big gig. I can just tell them to stop doing it." [33]

Instead of just producing enlightenment, however, the bit also produced arrest:

> Now when I took the bust, I finished the show. I said that word, you know, the ten-letter word. And the heat comes over and says, "Uh, Lenny, my name is Sergeant Blah-blah. You know that word you said?"
>
> "I said a lotta words out there."
>
> "Well, that, that word."
>
> "Oh, yeah."
>
> "Well, Lenny, that's against the law, an' I'm gonna take ya down."
>
> "O. K. That's cool."
>
> "It's against the law to say it and to do it."
>
> "But I didn't do it, man."
>
> "I know, but, uh, I just have to tell you that, all the time."
>
> "O. K." [34]

As was only to be expected, the arrest had more than its share of irony, to say nothing of official hypocrisy. For one thing, police and court officials alike were completely insensitive to the point Lenny had been trying to make; like the booking agent in his scenario, they insisted on associating the word "cocksucker" (here disguised as "blah-blah-blah" so as to enable Bruce to avoid subsequent arrests) exclusively with homosexual practices:

> They said it was vernacular for a favorite homosexual practice. That's weird how they manifested that word as homosexual, 'cause I don't. That relates to any contemporary chick I know, or would know, or would love, or would marry. [35]

For another, while the police and district attorney browbeat Lenny unmercifully for using "cocksucker" in a public place, testimony during the trial established that it was frequently used in the police station itself. [36] But the crowning touch was that, now that Lenny had given them an excuse, the officials themselves actually *enjoyed* saying the word:

> Now, in court. The judge, Aran Abramitz [Albert Axelrod], a red-headed junkyard Jew, a real *farbissener* [grim character], with thick fingers and a homemade glass eye. Tough-o, right? He comes in: "Blah-blah. Siddown."
> Swear the heat in: "What did he say?"
> "Your Honor, he said blah-blah-blah."
> *The judge*: "He said *Blah-blah-blah!*"
> Then the guy really *yenta*-ed [hammed] it up: "That's right. I didn't believe it. There was a guy up on the stage in front of women and a mixed audience saying blah-blah-blah."
> *The judge*: "This I never heard, blah-blah-blah. He said blah-blah-blah?"
> [*Witness*]: "He said blah-blah-blah! I'm not gonna lie to ya."
> It's in the minutes—"I'm not gonna lie to ya."
> Alright.

The D.A.: "The guy said blah-blah-blah. Look at him. He's smug, he's not gonna repent."

Then I dug something: they sort of liked saying blah-blah-blah. Because they said it a few extra times.

Now, they really got so involved saying blah-blah-blah, the bailiff is yelling, "What'd he say?"

"Shut up, you blah-blah-blah."

They were yelling it in the court: "Whad'ya gonna blah-blah-blah."

"Goddamn! It's good to say blah-blah-blah."[37]

As can be seen from the foregoing, his approach to demystifying language so as to be able to discuss any subject rationally was, for all its personal risks to Lenny, potentially a most fruitful one — even, to a certain extent, with judges, district attorneys, and bailiffs. Bruce also had several even more audacious monologues and bits that dealt with sexual concepts. One of the most celebrated of these also played a prominent role in his San Francisco "obscenity" trial:[38]

[*In falsetto*] Toooooo is a preposition.

[*Hits cymbal*] To is a preposition.

[*Hits drums*] Come is a verb.

[*Very rapidly*] To is a preposition. Come is a verb.

To is a preposition.

Come is a verb, the verb intransitive.

To come.

To come.

I've heard these two words my whole adult life, and as a kid when I thought I was sleeping.

To come.

To come.

It's been like a big drum solo.

Did you come? [*hits drum*]

Did you come? [*hits cymbal*]

[*Faster, hitting drums and cymbals for emphasis*]

Did you come *good*?

Did you come *good*?

Did you *come* good?

Did you come good?
Did you come good?
Did you *come* good?
Did you *come* good?
I come better with you, sweetheart
than anyone
in the whole goddamned world.
Woman's voice: I really came *so* good.
I really came *so* good, 'cause I love you.
I really came so good.
I come better with you, sweetheart,
than anyone in the whole world.
I really came so good.
So good.
But don't come in me. [*Hits tom-tom*]
Don't come in me. [*Hits snare drum*]
[*Singing, in march cadence*] Don't come in me, mim-mim-mim-me
Don't come in me, mim-mim-mim-me
Don't come in me.
[*Slowly*]
Don't come in me, mim-me.
Don't come in me, mim-me. 39

On occasion, Bruce at this point might interject a (fictional) recitative:

My sister bled to death in the back of a taxicab from a bad curettage, because she had a baby in her belly. She was a tramp—my father said she was a tramp, because the witch doctor didn't put a hoop on her finger. That's why she bled to death in the back of that taxicab—'cause she couldn't come home with a baby in her belly, a tramp with life in her stomach. So don't come in me, unless you want to kill me. 40

[*Hitting cymbal*] *Man's voice:* I can't come.
Woman's voice: 'Cause you don't love me, that's why you can't come.

Man: I love you, I just can't come—that's my hang-up. I can't come when I'm loaded, all right?

Woman: 'Cause you don't love me.

Man: Just what the hell is the matter with you? What has that got to do with loving? I just can't come, that's all. [41]

And then he might add:

Man: Awright! Awright. You want me to tell you why? I'm gonna tell you the truth: You know why we never had any kids? 'Cause I can't come, 'cause it's DIRTY! All that bullshit in the books, but it ain't in that Sunday book, because . . . good people don't come. And I'm gonna rise above the physical, the carnal—don't you think I'm ashamed of coming? It's filthy and rotten. And I'm just sorry they blamed it on you. That's why we never had any kids; but they blamed it on you and kept you in bed with those dumb temperature charts. So if you want kids, you better get a different old man. But I sure do love you. But I just can't help it—intellectual awareness does me no good. I know it's not dirty but it is dirty. You know what I mean? God damn it! Oh shit! Maybe we oughta adopt some kid from some bum who can come. [42]

[*Bruce's own voice*]: Now if anyone in this room, or the world, finds those two words decadent, obscene, immoral, amoral, asexual—the words "to come" really make you feel uncomfortable, if you think I'm rank for saying it to you, you the beholder gets ranked from listening to it—you probably can't come! [43]

There are, in addition, a few other of Lenny's bits that merit examination in the context of efforts at de-conditioning adults who have been indoctrinated to believe that sex and the human body are somehow "dirty." The first of these was an extension of Bruce's proposition that "if anyone . . . believes that God made his body, and [that] body is dirty, the fault lies with the manufacturer. It's that cold, Jim."[44] The bit, as performed in Chicago, where it won Bruce another "obscenity" arrest (in 1962), begins with his holding up a picture of a naked woman and asking his audience, "How can that pretty lady be indecent?" From there, Bruce turns to "tramps" (who "get their just deserts by bleeding to death in the back of taxicabs"), and from there, to the sex act:

> How about *doing it*, how do you feel about that, you people, is that about the dirtiest thing we could do to each other? Priests don't do it, nuns don't do it, Patamonza Yoganunda doesn't do it, rabbis are close to celibacy — it's really not very nice, is it, *doing it* . . .? [People begin to leave.] . . . Before all of you escape, let me explain something to you. You see, you defeat your purpose. It's God, your filthy Jesus Christ, [who] made these tits, that's all. Now you've got to make up your mind, you've got to stand up to Jesus, and you've got to say, "Look, I admit that *doing it* is filthy, I will stop doing it." And, believe me, if you'll just set the rules, I will obey them. But . . . stop living the paradox. Tell me that it's filthy, that fags are the best people; I will live up to the misogynist, I will be the woman-hater, I will be the nice guy that takes your daughter out. "He's a nice guy, he didn't try to fool around with me, he was a nice faggot."[45]

The second of these bits grew gradually out of Bruce's exposure to the law in First Amendment court cases involving "obscenity." Bruce was convicted of this charge in Chicago, and the Illinois Supreme Court unanimously upheld his conviction. It was only overturned as a result of the U. S. Supreme Court decision in the case of *Jacobellis v. State of Ohio* (1964).[46] As Lenny explained that decision:

> The obscenity law, when everything boils away, is: Does it appeal to the prurient interest?
> I must get you horny — that's what it means.
> If I do a *disgusting* show — a show about eating pork — that's not obscene. Although you Jews and

vegetarians and Moslems will bitch your asses off,
that's my right as an American, to talk about pork,
to extol its virtues, to run in front of a synagogue,
yelling: "Here's pork! Look at it, rabbi!"

"Get him out of here, he ought to be arrested — that's
disgusting!"

It doesn't matter. . . . If a guy wants to wail with
pork, that's his *schtick* [bit].

Or, if I do a vulgar show . . . wear platform shoes,
Kitty Kellys with ankle straps — it's not obscene.

No, obscenity has only one meaning: to appeal to
the prurient interest. [47]

Bruce's question was the obvious one:

What's wrong with appealing to the prurient interest?
We appeal to the *killing* interest. [48]

I really want the Supreme Court to stand up and
tell me that fucking is dirty and no good. [49]

It was following on this line of reasoning that Lenny
retrospectively concluded that he would have preferred "to
fight the Chicago obscenity rap on a whole different issue"
— on the issue he raised with his question, "What's *wrong*
with appealing to the prurient interest?" [50] As an immediate
case in point, Bruce argued:

. . . I would rather my child see a stag film than
The Ten Commandments or *King of Kings* — because
I don't want my kids [to learn] to kill Christ when
he comes back. That's what they see in those films —
that violence.

Bruce then performed the monologue that presumably he
would deliver to children viewing their first "dirty movie,"
as he termed it:

All right, kids, sit down now, this picture's gonna
start. It's not like *Psycho*, with a lot of four-letter
words, like "kill" and "maim" and "hurt" — but you're

gonna see this film now and what you see will probably impress you for the rest of your lives, so we have to be very careful what we show you. . . . Oh, it's a dirty movie. A couple is coming in now. I don't know if it's gonna be as good as *Psycho,* where we have the stabbing in the shower and the blood down the drain. . . . Oh, the guy's picking up the pillow. Now, he'll probably smother her with it, and that'll be a good opening. Ah, the degenerate, he's putting it under her ass. Jesus, tsk, tsk, I hate to show this crap to you kids. All right, now he's lifting up his hand, and he'll probably strike her. No, he's caressing her, and kissing her — ah, this is disgusting! All right, he's kissing her some more, and she's saying something. She'll probably scream at him, "Get out of here!" No, she's saying, "I love you, I'm coming." Kids, I'm sorry I showed you anything like this. God knows this will be on my conscience the rest of my life — there's a chance that [now] you may do this when *you* grow up. Well, just try to forget what you've seen. Just remember, what this couple did belongs written on the wall of a men's room. And, in fact, if you ever want to do it, do it in the men's room.

Then, almost as an afterthought, Bruce added: "I never did see one stag film where anybody got killed in the end. Or even slapped in the mouth."[51]

If anybody deserves the spiritual credit for inspiring the slogan "Make Love Not War," it would have to be Lenny Bruce. Yet although Bruce, for reasons I have sought to elucidate previously, did devote considerable effort to undermining authoritarian ideologies that promoted sexual repression and irrational thinking generally, that was by no means the totality, or even the most important focus, of his work. Rather, Bruce turned his extremely fertile wit and incredibly quick and retentive mind to just about every form of socially sanctioned but logically untenable ideology. In what follows, I will try to touch on what I consider some of the more important areas in which Bruce pitted his reasoning against the conventional wisdom.

Narcotics. For hard-core addicts of the defective and contrary-to-fact syllogism, smoking the "narcotic" marijuana inevitably leads to injecting heroin, Bruce (who himself did not smoke)[52] had a simple but telling counter-proposition:

> *First convict:* I'm a strung-out junkie. I started smoking pot, that's the way I started. By the way, cellmate, how did you get to be a murderer of eighteen people and the horrible gambler that you are?
> *Second convict:* I started gambling with bingo in the Catholic Church.
> *First convict:* I see. [53]

Crackpot realism,[54] *reflex patriotism, and the cold war.* The key to understanding Lenny Bruce's position on all political issues, the cold war most unequivocally included, is the realization that he was not in any sense a liberal. Thus in a period when liberals — not least among them Jewish liberals — were joining in the hysterical howling for the lives of Julius and Ethel Rosenberg, in a case that smells increasingly fishy and concocted as it recedes in time,[55] Lenny had somewhat of a different understanding of the issues involved:

> Goddamn the priests and the rabbis. Goddamn the Popes and all their hypocrisy. Goddamn Israel and its bond drives. What influence did they exert to save the lives of the Rosenbergs — guilty or not? . . . [T]he Ten Commandments doesn't say, "Thou Shalt Not Kill *Sometimes* . . ."[56]

For Lenny, human life loomed larger than ideology, and such slogans as "Better Dead than Red" comprised the *real* obscenity. His response (implicitly) to the super-patriots and ideological fanatics who condemned U-2 pilot Francis Gary Powers for not taking his own life when his plane was downed over the Soviet Union in 1960 was to point out to these zealots that talk comes exceedingly cheap when it is not your own life that is being laid on the line:[57]

Would you sell out your country? Who comes first,
you or your country? I don't have to think twice;
I know me, Jim — the flag goes right down the toilet!
And I will not try to live up to the perversion of what
should be, because it never existed. And if *you* would
not, then you cop the thousand dollars. The culture
teaches, "Cast the first stone," 'cause you know, well,
maybe you're not that good, but there are those good
men, and good men should exist, so burn his ass when
I'm the chairman of the jury. That's it, Jim.

Here are the top secrets; look in the [unintelligible],
right here. The top secrets: "You wouldn't sell your
country out?"

"Never, I'm a cryptographer. The secrets — I'll never
give them up, no matter what. What are they doing to
that other guy? They got his pants down. What are
they putting that funnel in his ass for? I don't know.
I don't care. I would never sell my country out. What
are they heating up that lead for? They're not gonna
put that lead in the funnel that's in his ass, are they?
They did. [Whistles] Bullshit! Here's the secrets, Jim."

I'm gonna *make up* secrets. But don't pour the hot
lead in my ass, Mister. That's it.

If you can take the hot lead enema, then you can
cast the first stone. [58]

Perhaps the single greatest index of Lenny's independence
of thought is manifested in the fact that, unlike virtually
everyone else of his generation (he was forty at the time
of his death in August 1966), [59] he never succumbed to
the massive doses of cold war hysteria that were unleashed
upon the U. S. public from above after World War II.
Hence he was able to reject out of hand all forms of
anticommunist intervention, whether military or ideological; witness his comments on Radio Free Europe and the
ludicrous notion of "rolling back" Communist govern-
ments in the name of "freedom," when freedom does not
exist here:

I'm not gonna buy any time for Radio Free Europe.
Frig that. Yeah, the disc jockey: "And that was the

Coasters on the flip side of 'Two Up and Two Back and the Hully Gully,' and how bad do you hate Communism? Why don't you lay some bread on us, and Radio Free Europe, and blah-blah."

Why not? 'Cause I have nothing to tell Europe, man, at all. All I can tell Europe is that, ah, this is my country and I dig it here, it's good to me, and there's no right or wrong. It's mine—that's all. I'm not gonna moralize with you. If communism cooks for you, solid, man. But I'm not gonna try to *free* anybody. Not when the governor of Georgia closed the schools. Nah, I can't tell 'em—what is that? It's dopey talk, already. Not right or wrong—it cooks for me.

And people talk about *freedom.* You know, I can go anywhere in Europe tonight, I'd walk in any country, I don't need a visa. But I would shit to walk in Mississippi with a sign on my back: "I'm from New York, Ha, Ha, Ha."[60]

Lenny also had the temerity to think the unthinkable, scoffing at the ultimate orthodoxy, that the cold war had resulted from a noble U.S. response to villainous Red aggression, as in this short example taken from one of a series of parody political speeches he composed:[61]

> *Politician:* "We have never been, and never will be, a warlike nation. We demand Russia disarm."
> *Bruce:* That's pretty wild.[62]

Politics, Black people and the limitations of liberalism. In speaking of the difference between Mort Sahl and Lenny Bruce, Kenneth Tynan astutely notes that:

> The election of John F. Kennedy robbed Sahl of most of his animus, which had been directed toward Eisenhower from the lame left wing of the Democratic Party. It became clear that Bruce was tapping a vein of satire that went much deeper than the puppet warfare of the two-party system. Whichever group was in power, his criticisms remained valid.[63]

As Tynan's remarks suggest, the essence of Bruce's approach to politics was that it transcended the usual cliches of Democratic Party, lesser-of-two-evils liberalism. Instinctively, Bruce went directly to the heart of the matter, the sham nature of the two-party system:

> I don't get involved with politics as much as Mort Sahl does, because I know that to be a [successful] politician . . . you must be what all politicians have always been: chameleonlike. [64]

> I grew up in New York, and I was hip as a kid that I was corrupt and that the mayor was corrupt. I have no illusions.
> You believe politicians, what they say? It's a device to get elected. If you were to follow Stevenson from New York to Alabama you would shit from the changes.
> It's like two syndicates, man. . . . But morals don't enter into it. [65]

Since two presidents have been elected within less than a decade on a platform of promising peace only to bring an expansion and prolongation of war—not to mention such illustrious predecessors as Woodrow Wilson and Franklin D. Roosevelt—Bruce's warning ought to strike a responsive chord among historians and political scientists.

As cases in point of the corrupt nature of the political *system*, Bruce took the careers of Jimmy Walker, William O'Dwyer, Sherman Adams, and Bernard Goldfine. Walker was "a heavy *gonif* [thief], a master *gonif*, man. . . . [T]hey *really* punished him—Bob Hope did his life . . . O'Dwyer they really gave it *hais* [hot] to—he moved to Mexico. As the ambassador." Once O'Dwyer returned to New York, moreover, he spent his time

> just laying on the floor laughing his ass off. That's it. Jail is for poor people. Cause Sherman Adams and St. Bernard [Goldfine] never sat in the joint, man. Cause it's juice [power], man. That's it. The only rights that you got are knowing the right guy. [66]

To illustrate the cynical nature of U. S. political leadership, Bruce conceived of several imaginary speeches that
could be used by candidates for high public office. Two in
particular are not only accurate reflections of his views
but, alas, of reality as well: [67]

> Now we got a speech if the other party wins. We give
> the president a speech where we wanna be a nice guy —
> but still give the other party the shaft, you know:
>   *Politician:* Regardless of party, we're all one. One
> for one common good as Americans. We shall help
> the other party in every way, to keep from heading
> to the inevitable path of chaos and depression to
> which they will lead us.
>   Now for people who want war, people who don't
> want war, people who are pro-segregation, pro-integra-
> tion, Little Rock, the whole scene. It's called "Safety
> First." This one's a capper:
>   *Second politician:* In this country, regardless of race,
> color or creed, the color has a right to know, it be-
> comes everyone's duty. The duty that has become the
> right of every man, woman, and child. A child that
> one day will be proud of his heritage, a child that
> only in these perilous times, when a man-born menace,
> a horrible bomb, that can only disfigure and defame
> its creator, a horror, an evil, a bad, a lazy, a lethar-
> gic. [*Tone becomes increasingly strident*] Lethargy and
> complacency we cannot fall into. We've got a bomb
> that can wipe out half the world if necessary. And
> we will! To keep our standards, the strength that has
> come from American unity, that we alone will build,
> for better schools and churches. [68]

Bruce was therefore somewhat disdainful of the conventional liberal pieties, especially when liberals themselves
displayed no little hypocrisy:

> The liberals are so liberal that they can't understand
> the bigots:
>   "I'm so understanding. I can't understand anyone
> not understanding me, as understanding as I am." [69]

Bruce sometimes expanded this bit in greater detail:

> "I'm so liberal I've never had any *rachmones* [sympathy] for the white Southerner—'He tawks lahk that, he tawks lahk that'—"
> The poor *schmuck* probably doesn't even talk like that, but some *schmuck* in the Bronx wrote a screenplay with him 'tawkin lahk that' so the *putz* ends up 'tawkin lahk that.'[70]

This theme of sympathy for the white Southerner—definitely at odds with the usual liberal verities—was one Bruce was to repeat often and in many contexts and variants, in the process displaying his own considerable ability to *hab rachmones* (have compassion) for any group or person in need of it. Here, for instance, is his imaginative, insightful and highly empathetic account of a Ku Klux Klan leader—at first glance, a rather unlikely object for *rachmones*—forced to testify in front of a congressional committee:[71]

> When a guy joined the Ku Klux Klan, I'm sure that he didn't say: "I solemnly swear that I'll lynch people and I'll murder." No. It's the same scene as the communist writers. That witch-hunt. There were some writers, you know, that probably knew nothing about communism, and in order to get a gig—you know, like people join the Shriners or play golf to meet different people—had some association with this organization (this is 'way, 'way back). Then they have like the House Un-American Activities Committee. They *grabbed* everybody up—you know, all these writers—and they said, the fact that the *Communist* Party—*the* communists, overthrow the government—the fact that these people had anything to do with it at one time in their lives, even talk to some cat, that just blew it for them.
> Well, the same thing with the Ku Klux Klan. The fact that one Ku Klux Klan member lynched somebody sometime, some poor asshole now gets *schlepped* [dragged] up before the House Un-American Activities

Committee, who doesn't know about anything — all he
wanted to do was sell some used car to a guy in Tennessee.

Member of HUAC: Were you ever a member of the
Klan?

The fact this cat didn't graduate high school really
puts him uptight. The [Imperial] Wizard now. Because
it's really weird, when if you're on the stand, you're
just dragged in front of it, you know, and: "Were you
ever, were you ever? . . ."

He doesn't understand the North, this cat, at all.
The last time he did any signing or admitting anything,
the carpetbaggers really screwed him out of everything.

So he just, [Robert] Shelton [KKK Imperial Wizard],
he doesn't want to admit he's an American citizen,
even: "Decline, decline, decline, decline."

The South . . . you know, we pissed away a million
dollars on Radio Free Europe and never gave them a
nickel. [72]

So in addition to his unwillingness to worship at the
pantheon of the approved deities, Lenny Bruce also
violated liberal protocol by refusing to hate the socially
sanctioned scapegoats.

With typical Bruce perception, Lenny readily grasped
the fact that all the crucial issues of domestic politics
during the 1960s would be raised by the Black movement for human rights. Just as quickly, he noted that the
liberal approach — integration — was fatally flawed by
white condescension and paternalism, and was thus
doomed to fail. He was too intimately involved with Black
people — they comprised, he estimated at one point, about
30 percent of his audience[73] — not to know that they would
scarcely be grateful for tokenistic gestures on the part of
white liberals. In short, Bruce was able to anticipate the
rise of a Black Power movement that would not regard
such would-be "friends of the Negro" with anything remote-
ly resembling affection: "Liberal, schmiberal. Um, hm."
Nor would white liberals be exactly overjoyed at the development of Black Power: [74]

How many Negroes *are* there in this country? Maybe
census takers have screwed up a bit. I assume they
passed a few colored houses.

Census taker: I'm not goin' in those houses — bullshit! Just ask the kid. Hey, sonny, how many in this
block, here?

Old man: Well, I, uh, ah . . .

Census taker: Put it down, fifteen, that's it.

Now you see a vote will come in.

Man: What the hell is this? Three billion from Ala-
bama. Two million, six million. Where the hell are
these people comin' from?

The houses; they're all in tiers, waiting to vote — all
those Negroes.

That's really weird. The vote's changed a few things.
It's changed this: In one year you see an all-Black
jury, a Black judge — and shit!

White: They're all Black. How the hell you gonna
get a fair shake with an all-Black jury?

Bruce: You're not — ha-ha. What is, Jim. And a lotta
people like myself will say, "Wait a minute, I was a
liberal."

Black: I'm tired of hearin' that bullshit, you were
liberal.

Bruce: You don't understand me. I was with — I
was *before* Bayard Rustin. I was with Vito Marcan-
tonio. I *schlepped* my ass off — I'll show you canceled
checks —

Black: That's it — I don't wanna hear about it. I
don't want to hear about one more liberal. Every
German you talked to loved the Jews, and they're
all dead. Guilty by omission — forget it. [75]

If anything, Bruce heaped even more scorn on the at-
tempts of Hollywood liberals like Stanley Kramer to make
"relevant" motion pictures with integrationist themes.
Movies provided Bruce with raw material for some of
his most fruitful inventions; and many of those bits that
were not explicit parodies of movies were nonetheless cast
in the form of film scenarios. [76] Kramer's *The Defiant
Ones* was thus, by virtue of its absurd, implausible end-

ing (a Black escaped convict sacrifices his freedom in order to be returned to prison with his newly found white buddy), a doubly perfect vehicle for Bruce's wit (as assisted by Black guitarist Eric Miller): [77]

> *Bruce: The Defiant Ones.*
> *Escaped white convict:* Come on, Jane! Come on, Jane. Come out this way, Jane. This way, Jane.
> *Black convict (Randy):* Whaddayou keep calling me Jane for?
> *White:* You don' wanna be called "boy," do ya?
> *Black:* No.
> *White:* Boy, I tell ya somethin', Randy. My daddy would really whup me good if he ever heard me say this, but staindin' next to ya like this and bein' chained up to ya and havin' them hounds foller us — it's showed me somethin', it's opened up my eyes. You won't believe this, Randy, but it's taught me a lesson.
> *Randy:* What's that?
> *White:* I'm taller than you. An' bein' taller than you is a lesson in equality in itself.
> *Randy:* Speakin' of equality, I wonder if there'll ever be any equality?
> *White:* Why, there is Randy. Don't forget: to play *The Star-Spangled Banner*, it takes both the white keys and [pause] . . . the darkies. Randy, in fact, Randy, if you jus' think about it, jus' a liddle while, all that talk about equality — that's jus' a lotta nonsense. Why, evvruthin's equal, it's jus' people tryin' ta cause trouble. I tell ya why, Randy. Look, you ready for some examples? On equality?
> *Randy:* Uh hm.
> *White:* Now at income tax time, don't you get a chance to pay income tax same as evvribuddy else?
> *Randy:* Yeah.
> *White:* Thass equal, ain't it? Awright. Now, you gonna hol' up a store — don't you get the same time as ennybuddy else does?
> *Randy:* Yeah.
> *White:* Thass equal. Awright. Ready for the third one, heah? When it comes time for getting drafted

in the army, don't you get drafted along with evvri-
buddy else?
Randy: Yeah.
White: Well, thass equal.
Randy: Yeah, but, but—what about the schools and
the segregated housing?
White: Well, those things take a liddle time. Ya cain't
shove evvruthin' down people's throats there, Randy.
Now I wanna tell ya, heah. Someday, Randy, up
theah, up theah in Equality Heaven, they'll all be
theah Randy, the people who believe in it—Zanuck,
and Kramer. Thass why they make them pictures,
Randy, cause *they believe in equality*, Randy. An' up
theah, it's gonna happ'n, because they caused it to,
an'-an'-an'-an' then you gonna be livin' in Zanuck's
house with all yo' colored friends, and nex' door
to Kramer on his property in Malibu. An' you be
helpin' them people, Randy, polish dem cahs. [78]

Racism and public morality. Bruce was scathingly outspoken about the quasi-institutionalized nature of immorality in public life. Of the countless illustrations that
could be invoked, I have chosen two. The first of these
bits deals with the pervasive nature of white racism. In
1960, as a graduate student at Berkeley, I had the
pleasure of reviewing for the *Daily Californian* a performance of this piece by Bruce and Eric Miller at the
Masonic Auditorium in San Francisco. I would estimate
that roughly one-third of the audience was Black; two-
thirds were white; and of the latter, about one-half walked
out in high dudgeon during this portion of the performance. Apparently, Bruce was touching on widely
held attitudes that many (most?) whites were then either
unwilling or unable to confront in themselves: [79]

This is the typical white person's concept of how we
relax colored people at parties.
White: Eh, it's a hell of a spread—they really know
how to put on a treat, these people.
Black (Eric Miller): Yeah, it's very nice.
White: It's beautiful. I didn't get your name.

Black: Miller.

White: Miller, my name is [*mumbles unintelligibly*].

Black: Nice to meet you.

White: I never saw you around this neighborhood. Uh, you live around here?

Black: Uh, yeah. On the other side.

White: Oh, I was wonderin' about that. [*Pause*] That Joe Louis was a helluva fighter!

Black: Yeah.

White: Helluva man, helluva—there'll never be another Joe Louis. Uh, have ya gotta cigarette on ya?

Black: Yeah.

White: Uh, oh—the one you're smoking?! Uh, well, I'll put that out for ya, here. Ya know, I don't know these people too well. Are you familiar with them?

Black: No, it's uh . . .

White: I don't know if they're—I think they're Hebes—you're not Jewish, are ya? No offense! Some of my best friends are Jews. Have 'em over to the house for dinner. They're alright, uh, you know, some sheenies are no good, but you seem like a white Jew to me. Yeah, that Bojangles—Christ, could he tap dance!

Black: Oh, yeah . . .

White: You tap dance a little yourself, huh?

Black: Right, yeah . . .

White: All you people can tap dance, I guess. You people have a natural sense of rhythm. What's that, born right in ya, I guess, huh? Yeah, boy, way I figure it is, no matter what the hell a guy is, if he stays in his place, he's alright. That's the way I look at it. That's what's causin' all the trouble in the world—everybody, like, uh, I mean, uh—oh, here's to Joe Louis. Joe Louis was a guy who, the way I figure it, he was a guy just knew when to get in there and get out of there . . . that's more than I can say for a lotta you niggers. No offense—I had a few on the way over here, you know. You're alright; you're a good boy. Uh, did you have anything to eat yet?

Black: No, I haven't. I'm kinda hungry.

White: . . . if there's any watermelon left, uh, fried

chicken or dice or razors, but, uh, I'll see if I can
fix you up with somethin'. Uh, I wanna have you
over da house, but I've got a bit of a problem, now,
and I don't want you to think I'm out of line, but—
I gotta sister. And I hear that you guys—you know,
it's my sister, and . . . Well, I'll put it to you a dif-
ferent way: you wouldn't wan' no Jew doin' it to your
sister, wouldja? That's the way I feel about it, ya
know? I don't want no coon doin' it to my sister.
I didn't mean you no offense, ya know what I mean?
   Black: Sure.
   White: And as far as my sister's concerned, shake
hands on you won't do it to her.
   Black: Yeah.
   White: You won't do it to her?
   Black: No.
   White: I hear you got some perfume you put on,
when you—it'll make them do it to you.
   Black: No.
   White: You don't do it? It's not true? There's no
perfume you put on 'em? They just do it to ya?
   Black: No.
   White: You're awright. Hey, listen—uh, I'd like to
have you over to the house, I was tellin' ya, but,
uh, wait'll it gets dark, an', uh, . . .[80]

Typically, however, Bruce would not leave the matter
there, but would insist on bringing his rationalistic hu-
manism, or *rachmones*, into play:

The guy in this bit, we assume—see, that's the funny
thing about indictment—we assume that this cat is
all bad, then, and we destroy him. But you can't,
man. He's bad in this sense, [that] he has not ma-
tured, he has not been in a proper environment, 'cause
if he were to learn and to listen, he would swing,
'cause there are sensitive parts to him also, man. . . .
[T]he weird part [is] we get hung up with, "I am pure
and I am good, and those people are dirty and those
murderers are bad and I am so pure, I'm so good,
that I have to murder those murderers." And then
you end up getting screwed up. That's right.[81]

The second bit, "Christ and Moses,"[82] deals with Bruce's hilarious but telling indictment of the various ways in which organized religion tolerates and even rationalizes immorality in order not to alienate those with wealth and power. Lenny's basic premise was that "any man who calls himself a religious leader and owns more than one suit is a hustler as long as there is someone in the world who has no suit at all." Thus Bruce could conjecture, for example, that

> If Moses were to come down [from heaven], wouldn't he order all the rabbis in their Frank Lloyd Wright *shules* [temples] to sell their *tallith* [prayer shawls] for rags and melt down the *mezuzahs* for bail money for all the Caryl Chessmans who sit in gas chambers or electric chairs or walk in the blue-gray shadow of the gallows? Would not Moses say to them, "Why have you mocked the Ten Commandments? What is your interpretation of 'Thou Shalt Not Kill'? It's not, 'Thou Shalt Not Kill *But* . . .'"[83]

The recorded version of the descent of Christ and Moses is somewhat less sombre, but still makes the same point: the return of these two holy men would only serve to embarrass present-day religious spokesmen, who are in reality more concerned with temporal wealth and power than in implementing the professed precepts of Judeo-Christian morality.[84] We join Christ and Moses as they arrive on the West Coast:

> Okay, we go to the West Coast. See, there's all kinds of *shules*. Like West Coast, Christ and Moses will make Reform *shules* — Reform rabbis — so Reform they're ashamed they're Jewish. And they got a different sound. This is a typical Reform rabbi sound. Service — 12:01 Saturday night.
> *Rabbi* [*Harvard accent*]: And it should be said that the Children of Is-roy-el . . . ha, ha, Is-roy-el. Where is Is-roy-el? Is yonder Is-roy-el? Out quench yon flaming *yortseit* [memorial] candle, Is-roy-el. That is the Is-roy-el of cha-bel-yon David . . . and Ruth and Cherylanne and Joy!

Member of congregation: Oh, Rabbi! That was a beautiful speech.

Rabbi: Danksalot. Ya like dot? Vot duh hell—toochit top my head.

Member [incredulous]: Oh yeah?

Alright, now—Sunday. Christ and Moses fly to New York: "Trans-Continental, eighty-eight dollars to Chicago." Alright, now, let's see what they would make. They'd probably make—they say, "What's playin' at Saint Pat's?"

"Good double bill—Spellman and Sheen." "Oh, Mr. Spellman, Oh, Mr. Sheen, ta da ta da ta da . . . [*to the tune of "Gallagher and Shean"*].

Now, Christ and Moses are both possessed of humility. Why? Wisdom. That's it. Anybody who is secure, there's never any hostility, 'cause he's cool, yeah. Anyone who is above you, even, bingo, that's it. So they just stand in the back of Saint Patrick's. And they listen, look around. Cardinal Spellman would be relating love and giving and forgiveness to the people—and Christ would be confused. 'Cause their route took 'em through Spanish Harlem. And they would wonder what forty Puerto Ricans were doing living in one room—this guy had a ring on that was worth eight grand. And he would wonder at the grandeur . . . "Why aren't the Puerto Ricans living here—it's clean and nice? What does it all mean?" And they'd just be shucking back and forth and talking. And maybe Bishop Sheen would see them back there, and run up to Spellman on the lectern:

Sheen: Psssst. Wanna talk to you for a minute.

Spellman: Will you go back to the blackboard and stop bugging me now?

Sheen: I wanna talk to you. I've got a customer in the back.

Spellman: Awright, put the choir on for ten minutes.

Choir: Bah-ah-ah-ah-ah-ah.

Spellman: What is it?

Sheen: What is it?! You'll never guess who's here.

Spellman: Who's here?

Sheen: You're not going to believe me — you're gonna think I've been drinking.

Spellman: Awright, who's here?

Sheen: Christ and Moses.

Spellman: Are you putting me on now?

Sheen: I'm tellin' you they're here!

Spellman: Are you sure it's them?

Sheen: Well, I've just seen them in pictures, but I'm pretty sure it's them. Moses is a ringer for Charlton Heston, and I'm sure.

Spellman: Hmmm. Where are they standing?

Sheen: In the back — don't look now, you idiot, they can see us. Christ and Moses both here — they're way in the back there.

Spellman: Whew! Did Christ bring the family? What's his mother's name? Ummmmm . . . that's weird — I read the book today, too. I'm so nervous . . . ahhhhhh . . .

Sheen: Mary . . .

Spellman: Uh, Mary what?

Sheen: I don't know. Mary, uh, Mary Hail. No, Hail Mary — Mary Hail. Hail Mary? Hairy Mary? No — I don't know what the hell . . . oh, yeah, Hail Mary, alright, Hail Mary Full-of-Grace Thompson! They're very thick with the DuPonts out at Montauk Point.

Spellman: So they're back there?

Sheen: Yes.

Spellman: Ohhh, alright. That's something. If this ever gets around, now . . .

Sheen: It has. Oh, Christ! Don't look in the front door; the lepers are coming, alright. Uh, oh, yeah. [*Shouting*] Sir? Wouldja take the bell off, please? Thank you very much. Mister, would you pick up your leg — madame, your nose. You dropped it, thank you there. Awright.

Bruce: They got Sophie Tucker with Moses, posing!

Spellman: Take that Hebrew National banner down! Mr. Jessel, will you get off the Madonna, that's not a statue. Awright, gimme a direct line to Rome, quickly! Rome? Awright. Hello. John? Fran, in New York. Listen, a couple a kids dropped in and uh . . . yeah,

you know them. Well, I can't really talk right now—
excuse me.

Reporter: Hello, we're from *Newsweek*, and we
wanna know if they have State Department clearance,
and is that really them?

Spellman: Yes, it is them. Sonny! Get off my hem!
Yes, that is them, dear, yes. I don't know if they're
going to do any tricks today—I don't know. Yes,
they can fly. No, Mary Martin isn't God's Mother,
and get the hell out of here now! [*To the telephone*]
Hello? Ah, you know them. One kid is—well I'll
[*sings*] "With the cross of bap-bap." No, not Zorro!
Them! That's right. He brought a very attractive
Jewish boy with him. Well, we gotta do something.
What? No, I can't—put 'em up at your place! No,
I didn't paint or anything. I gotta lotta kids staying
over here. Look, what are we paying protection for?
That's right. Just get 'em over here, that's all. I don't
want to hear about that. Look, all I know is that
we're up to our ass in crutches and wheelchairs—is
that good enough for you? The place is *ridiculous*
here. Yeah, ah . . . they're in the back, way in the
back. *Of course they're white!!*[85]

If one had to choose a single word to describe the effect
that Lenny Bruce had on those who shared the moral
concern apparent in the foregoing material—keeping in
mind that as early as the beginning of the 1960s Bruce
was already dealing with the most controversial topics
that he would ever touch, and in the most expressive
language possible—that word would have to be
"liberating." This was particularly true for that generation
of young people. Earlier, I suggested that Bruce shared
certain similarities with Malcolm X. Some of these
similarities are relatively easy to discern. Both men were
charismatic figures and magnificently gifted orators (albeit in markedly different styles). Both men were essentially self-educated intellectuals (Bruce did not graduate
from high school), and all the more impressive for that.
Both had the courage to challenge in the name of justice
the most sacrosanct myths about the nature of U.S. so-

ciety. Both could be said to have been cut down in their prime for daring to express their outrage with the status quo in words of outspoken honesty and total commitment. Less immediately apparent but no less real, both men were to some degree the product of the Black jazz musicians' culture (an idea I shall develop at greater length as regards Bruce), which served to give them certain experiences, insights, and attitudes that are probably not to be had from any other source.[86] Both have been posthumously canonized, as it were, by their respective followers. And, just to make the parallel complete, Malcolm, like Lenny, now even has had his own off-Broadway production devoted to recounting his life and thought, *El Hajj Malik* (The Pilgrim Malcolm).[87]

What may be most significant in this context, however, is the fact that each man spoke — literally — for those who at the time had virtually no one else to voice their aspirations, frustrations, resentments, ideals. Malcolm, of course, sought to function on behalf of the Black rank and file — those whom Imamu Amiri Baraka (LeRoi Jones) so felicitously termed the "blues people." Bruce's constituency, if I may call it that, was somewhat different (although there was probably a certain amount of overlap with Malcolm's), and rather more amorphous as well. Be that as it may, my contention is that Lenny increasingly served as a major prophet for young cultural and political enemies of the status quo — that is, for the two groups that were subsequently to crystallize as the counter-culture on the one hand and the New Left on the other.

What evidence, other than personal recollection,[88] is there to substantiate such a claim? One might do worse than to begin by mentioning that Lenny Bruce posters now appear with absolute regularity beside those of Malcolm, Janis Joplin, Angela Davis, Jimi Hendrix, and so on in college book stores and head shops. It is also more than coincidence, I suspect, that the authors of both the Afterword to Lenny's autobiography, *How to Talk Dirty and Influence People*, and the Epilogue to *The Essential Lenny Bruce* advance the same argument that I am making here. John Cohen, editor and compiler of *The Essential Lenny Bruce*, maintains that "the only people who really dig Lenny Bruce are the people who are doing the same thing Bruce did—cutting loose, turning on, turning away [from the Establishment], trying to turn America around"; while Dick Schaap writes (with greater precision) of a memorial service held for Bruce in New York, attended by "people who suspected they were alone until, maybe six, seven years ago [1959-60], before Mississippi marches and draft-card barbecues, Lenny bound them all together." [89]

Still more specific are the cases of three Lenny Bruce freaks — the way followers of Bruce, using his lexicon, usually referred to themselves — from the West Coast, where Bruce's influence was, logically, probably at its greatest.

Phil Spector proclaimed himself "the first teen-age millionaire" on the David Susskind television program. Whatever the actual amount of his fortune at the time, Spector achieved it by becoming the first successful young producer of rock records aimed at the youth market; [90] he has since consolidated his attainments by producing records for the Beatles and, more recently, John Lennon and Yoko Ono. Spector went from an admirer of Bruce to an intimate friend — Bruce salutes him directly on *Lenny Bruce Is Out Again*, and mentions attending one of his parties on *The Berkeley Concert*— and in addition issued one of Bruce's last records on his own Philles label [91] at a time when Bruce found it next to impossible to obtain employment. When Bruce died in 1966, Spector took out an advertisement in a trade paper blaming his death on "an overdose of police," [92] as well as providing (anonymously) the money for Bruce's funeral.

Grace Slick is now known as the lead singer of the Jefferson Airplane. Prior to joining the Airplane, however, she worked with her then-husband Darby Slick in another San Francisco rock group, the Great Society. Some time after the breakup of that band, Columbia Records released two albums cut from tapes made around 1966. Featured on the first volume is Grace's rendition of "Father Bruce"; and, indicative of what I have described as the liberating effect that Lenny had on the development of the counter-culture (especially in San Francisco), she ends her performance of "Father Bruce" with a hearty exclamation of a notorious four-letter word. [93]

Frank Zappa is the brilliant composer, guitarist, and leader of one of the most interesting and innovative rock bands ever to play, the Mothers of Invention. Zappa, who shares a number of Bruce's characteristics (self-educated intellectual, harassment by censors, etc.), is a profound admirer of Bruce, whose influence is easily detectable in the lyrics that Zappa and his cohorts write for the Mothers. Like Phil Spector, Zappa has also issued an album of Bruce's material—in this case an entire performance, unexpurgated—on his appropriately named Bizarre label. [94] Furthermore, at one point Zappa was so taken with Bruce's work that he planned to intersperse some of Bruce's tapes with songs by the Mothers on an album that was to be called either *The Mothers and Lenny Bruce* or *Our Man in Nirvana,* although this project apparently never reached completion. [95]

It was precisely because Bruce appeared to be such a potent rallying point for young political and cultural dissenters from the conventional wisdom that he was perceived as a threat by Those In Command. To be sure, by comparison with forms of dissent that would come later—ghetto rebellions, massive protest marches involving hundreds of thousands, explicitly radical and even revolutionary political activity, antiwar organizing within the military, and the like—Lenny's merely verbal onslaughts against the status quo may seem a trifle tame. But to judge Lenny by such a standard would be nothing more than an extended exercise in unhistorical thinking. At the time Lenny was at his peak—roughly from 1960 to 1964, a period that, probably not coincidentally, includes most of his nineteen or more arrests [96]—few of these more massive protest activities had erupted through the surface. (The first ghetto insurrection of the 1960s, for instance, took place in Harlem in 1964.) Moreover, to a certain immeasurable but nonetheless very real extent, Lenny's work helped clear the decks for later waves of radical political opposition. The Berkeley Free Speech Movement, for instance (whose leaders subsequently turned up in the Vietnam Day Committee), the Yippies, and other militant left-wing groups were in all likelihood partially inspired by Lenny's own recurrent battles for free speech in the San Francisco Bay area.[97] By the standards of the day, Bruce's work constituted a potentially dangerous attempt to undermine the established order, and as a result Bruce was persecuted for it.

In *The Power Elite*, C. Wright Mills wrote that:

> It is much safer to celebrate civil liberties than to defend them; it is much safer to defend them as a formal right than to use them in a politically effective way. . . . It is easier still to defend someone else's right to have used them years ago than to have something yourself to say *now* and to say it now forcibly. The defense of civil liberties — even of their practice a decade ago — has become the major concern of many liberal and once leftward scholars. All of which is a safe way of diverting intellectual effort from the sphere of political reflection and demand.[98]

Lenny sought to use civil liberties "in a politically effective way" and to say something "*now* and say it forcibly." For his efforts he was rewarded with a near-incredible pattern of harassment and suppression, orchestrated by the Establishment agencies of what passes for law and order — the police, the courts, and the district attorneys.

In Chicago, for example, where the city administration is Catholic-dominated, Bruce was busted for alleged "obscenity" in December 1962. In reality, however, the consensus reached by objective students of Bruce's career — including, in this instance, *Variety* magazine — is that the arrest was a response to Bruce's strictures on society, including its repressive religious ideologies, rather than to any supposed "obscenities." The reporter for *Variety* (generally regarded as a politically conservative publication) wrote that "Bruce's comments on the Catholic Church have hit sensitive nerves in Chicago's Catholic-oriented administration and police department," and the prosecuting attorney was more "concerned with Bruce's indictments of organized religion [than] with the . . . sexual content of the comic's act."[99] Following the arrest, moreover, the police officer who swore out the complaint on Bruce returned to the supper club where he was playing to threaten the owner (according to the tape Lenny had running at the time) that, "speaking as a Catholic," the club's "license was in danger" so long as Bruce was employed there; and that the Chicago Police Department was "going to have someone watching every show." For the trial itself the city administration further mobilized Catholic power to insure a conviction: forty-seven members of a possible fifty on his jury panel were Catholic, and all twelve members of the final jury were Catholic, as were the judge, prosecuting attorney, and the prosecutor's assistant. On Ash Wednesday, each one of these fifteen people came into court with a spot of ash on his or her forehead. And so it went; Bruce's conviction was automatic. And shortly after Bruce left Chicago, the club where he had been performing at the time of his arrest "lost its liquor license and the owner had to sell out." [100]

By way of contrast, the prosecuting attorneys in his New York "obscenity" trial in 1964 later revealed that they believed Lenny innocent of violating the law — but decided to press charges against him anyway. Testifying in the capacity of expert witnesses for the prosecution, moreover, were such Establishment literary big guns as John Fischer, then editor of *Harper's*, Marya Mannes of *The Reporter*, and, naturally, the obligatory minister. A three-judge panel concluded by a two to one vote that Lenny was guilty, and the *New York Law Journal* decided not to publish the decision on the grounds that "without . . . deletions[,] publication was impossible within the *Law Journal* standards." Needless to emphasize, the *New York Law Journal*'s response helped in prejudicing the climate against Lenny even further. [101]

Bruce's conviction and sentencing for an alleged "narcotics" violation in Los Angeles (1963-64) reveals the same pattern of flagrant bias. The police sergeant who arrested Bruce and whose testimony convicted him was himself under suspicion at the time of the trial; shortly thereafter he was sentenced to a five-year term in federal prison for illegal importation of narcotics. [102] One of the two court-appointed doctors who testified against Bruce in his sen-

tencing hearing—that Bruce would be found guilty by a
jury was never in doubt after the lurid publicity in the
Los Angeles newspapers—had been, as stated before,
dismissed from his post in a Tennessee hospital for castrat-
ing a patient against his will and other forms of incompetence. The other doctor stated that he had signed a certificate declaring Bruce to be a narcotics addict after only
a cursory examination and prior to any expert testimony
in the sentencing hearing, and that he "would still sign the
certificate" even if he "had heard a dozen witnesses testify"
that Bruce was not an addict. Several physicians who were
knowledgeable in the area of addiction did in fact testify
that Bruce was not an addict, foremost among them Dr.
Joel Fort, who is now nationally recognized for his outstanding research in the field. Notwithstanding all of these
mitigating circumstances—the tainted nature of the
prosecution's case against Bruce, the obvious prejudice
of the court-appointed doctors, the impressive expert testimony marshaled by Bruce's attorneys to show that he
was not addicted to heroin—the judge, who could have
given Bruce a two-year sentence, instead gifted him with
ten. [103]

The aim of this campaign of Establishment harassment,
in my opinion, was to throttle Bruce by preventing him
from performing in public. And, regardless of the fact
that Bruce ultimately won acquittal in all but one of the
cases in which he stood trial (the Los Angeles "narcotics"
arrest)—and continued to maintain his innocence even in
that one—throttle him it did. At one point, Bruce could
count some nineteen arrests on various charges. Busts
came so frequently that the circumstances they produced
far surpassed the merely ludicrous. For instance, the con-
dition put on his bail in one of several Los Angeles arrests
prevented him from appearing in Chicago for sentencing
in his "obscenity" trial! [104] This situation had its humorous
aspects; others, however, were less funny. In the middle of
his judicial time of troubles, Lenny was offered a lucrative
position as a television scriptwriter—only to have it with-
drawn again because, in view of his numerous busts,
his morals were not felt to be up to the high standards
of the television industry. [105]　Absurd? Bizarre? Certainly.

Funny? Hardly. Or again, after playing in Detroit "for almost eight years," Bruce was

> due to open at The Alamo in March 1964, but when the Detroit Board of Censors learned of this, they wouldn't permit my appearance — depriving me of my rights without even so much as a judicial proceeding.

Lenny also tried "calling up night-club owners all over the country, but they're all afraid to book me"; and "*Variety*, the Bible of Show Business, refuses [even] to accept an ad from me that simply states I'm *available*." [106]
The purpose of the deluge of persecution visited upon Bruce was explained, and with admirable succinctness at that, by the Illinois Supreme Court, which had originally — and unanimously — upheld his conviction for "obscenity" in Chicago. As a result of the U.S. Supreme Court decision in the case of *Jacobellis* v. *State of Ohio*, which ruled that no work could be found obscene unless it was utterly devoid of social significance, the Illinois Supreme Court was now, in its own words, "*constrained* to hold that the judgment of the circuit court of Cook County [i.e., Chicago] must be reversed and defendant [Bruce] discharged" (emphasis added). But the distinguished jurists from Illinois were clearly reluctant to reach this decision:

> . . . [W]e would not have thought that constitutional guarantees necessitate the subjection of society to the *gradual deterioration of its moral fabric which this type of presentation promotes.* . . . [107]

In other words, if it becomes necessary to choose between free speech that is supposedly protected by the Constitution on one hand, and preserving the "moral fabric" of the social order from the rational examination that Bruce conducted on the other — then so much the worse for free speech and the Constitution! Lenny himself phrased the matter more cogently when he wrote:

> They're really saying that they're only sorry the crummy Constitution won't permit them to convict me, but if they had *their* choice . . . [108]

But it wasn't necessary for Bruce's convictions to be upheld in order for them to accomplish the goal of silencing him. The seemingly endless series of arrests, trials, appeals, new arrests, and new trials exhausted Lenny's funds; and the de facto ban on employing him (even as a writer, much less a performer) prevented him from raising fresh funds. By October 1965, Bruce, who at one time had been able to command fees of $3,500 per week, was forced to declare himself legally bankrupt. [109] Thus at one stroke he was compelled to shift gears from an offensive assault upon a corrupt and immoral status quo to a defensive rearguard action in the courts. And thus society was narrowly rescued from "the gradual deterioration of its moral fabric which this type of presentation promotes."

If, in order to save the social order from such a threat, a life or two must be expended in the process, what, after all, is a mere human life? The incessant court battles plus the denial of opportunities to work did not merely hamstring Bruce. Together with a few judiciously timed, warrantless invasions of his house by the Los Angeles Police Department ("Here's my warrant," said one of L. A.'s finest, brandishing his pistol in Lenny's face), they actually started to erode his stability, as he himself recognized. [110] Lenny needed to work, we may hazard a guess, for more reasons than simply the financial ones. Performing inspired him in his most daring and creative thinking. Cut off from employment, he increasingly became obsessed with his legal defense, most likely in the hope that vindication by the courts would make it possible for him to appear in public once more. The details surrounding his death have never been clear (another parallel with Malcolm X, it might be noted in passing), and there isn't much to be gained by trying to sift the farrago of fact and rumor that began circulating before Lenny was even in the ground. Suffice it to say that his circumstances — no money, no chance to work, an incredibly large number of prolonged legal struggles looming on the horizon, to say nothing of several prison sentences hanging over his head, with recurrent rounds of breaking and entering by the Los Angeles police tossed in for good measure — these circumstances would probably have resulted in the death of individuals whose physical stamina was far greater than frail Lenny's was. [111]

But even as the very mortal Lenny Bruce was being efficiently and "legally" murdered, another chapter in the saga of Lenny Bruce the phenomenon was being written.

That such a thing as Lenny Bruce the phenomenon did come into existence is a tribute both to his ideas and the skill and intelligence with which Lenny presented them.

The phenomenon, however, is one that is shot through with paradox and contradiction. The city where his performances were held to be "obscene" — New York — has since had two stage production portraying his art, his life, his death. People who could have been relied upon to be among the first to walk out in the middle of one of his performances now want to be the first in their social circle to have seen him depicted on the stage. Even the academicians, who might have been dismayed or offended by an exposure to Bruce's work at first hand while he was alive, congregate solemnly to discuss the meaning and significance of that work now that he is dead.

Such are some of the more obvious paradoxes. They reflect others that lie beneath the surface. It was, as I have said, Bruce's penchant for the truth in his terms — let the chips fall where they may — that accounted for both his ever-growing following (especially among the young), and the equally growing wave of persecution and vilification to which he was subjected. His ideas were so explosive, his skill in presenting them so formidable, his ability to win followers so great, that he was marked out for destruction (at the very least, economic destruction through denial of the chance to perform) as a dangerous man. The more successful Bruce became at reaching and moving his audience, the closer he came to signing his own death warrant.

But the supreme contradiction is that the very act of snuffing out Bruce's life helped give posthumous currency to his words — and to his ideas. By compelling Bruce to become a martyr — much against his will, let it quickly be added, since Lenny had no taste for such a fate [112] — his persecutors also helped make him a hero. This was particularly true, as I have said, for youthful political and cultural dissidents. While his frontal assault on the leading repressive, authoritarian, and irrational ideologies

of the status quo was hardly a complete success for
Lenny personally, it unquestionably helped hasten the
more overt challenges that were being launched even as
he was being pushed prematurely into his grave. Many
of the values for which he risked and ultimately sacri-
ficed his own life have begun to triumph with the onset
of a new generation—the generation that is causing the
memory of Lenny Bruce to live on after the man himself is gone. In this way, Lenny starts to emerge vic-
torious over his adversaries; and his victory can only
become more secure with the passage of time. [113]

The fact that Lenny is now being eulogized in front
of the footlights testifies more vividly than anything
else to the powerful effect he has had on the generation
that came to maturity during the last decade. Not only
are these comparatively young people resurrecting his
life and his work but, by sheer weight of numbers, they
have made the subject of Lenny Bruce a "respectable"
one for their elders as well. Operating here is a well-known
principle of dialectics: with a change in quantity at a
certain point comes a change in quality. When enough
people subscribe to a heresy, it ceases to *be* heresy. In
this way—as with the cold war, the U.S. in Vietnam,
integration versus Black nationalism, marijuana, sexual
relations without marriage, the status of women in society, the laws on abortion, and countless other topics—
it has finally become possible to think the unthinkable
about Lenny Bruce: that he was right after all, that the
conventional wisdom is—bullshit.

Typically, Lenny was able to anticipate some of the
changes that young people would seek to bring about: [114]

> Now lemme tell you something about pot. Pot will
> be legal in ten years. Why? Because in this audience
> probably every other one of you knows a law student
> that smokes pot—who will become a senator, who
> will legalize it to protect himself. [115]

What he probably could not envision, of course, was the
importance of his own role as a catalyst in accelerating
those changes; or the fact that, dialectically—and ap-

propriately—his own stature would benefit from the changes that he himself was helping to precipitate.

Whatever consolation this may bring to Lenny's admirers, it probably would not have overjoyed Lenny himself, if for no other reason than the fact that he wasn't especially comfortable in the role of martyr *cum* hero. To Lenny, fighting his persecution—a word he wrote in quotation marks when he referred to himself—seemed as futile

> . . . as asking Barry Goldwater to speak at a memorial to send the Rosenberg kids to college. . . .
> I mean, when I think of all the crap that's been happening to me, the thing that keeps me from getting really outraged or hostile at the people involved is—and I'm sure that Caryl Chessman . . . felt this, too—that in the end, the injustice anyone is subjected to is really quite an *in* matter. [116]

With Lenny, you could have no doubt that the pun was intentional.

To the last, he retained his characteristic ability to discover some particle of the humorous or the bizarre in any situation—even his own. It is therefore only appropriate to let him compose his own epitaph, as it were, by putting even his passion for creating a just society under the same ironic and faintly mocking scrutiny that he applied to every other topic. In this way, as in so many others, the last laugh may truly be Lenny's:[117]

> [*Sung like chime notes*] Boom . . . Boom . . . Boom. WOR, the Bamberger Broadcasting System, and it's time for: HHHIIIYYYOOO, SIILLVERRR, AWAY.
> *First voice:* Hey, that guy didn't wait for a "Thank you."
> *Second voice:* He never does. That's the Masked Man. The Lone Ranger. He just likes people.
> *First voice* [*changing to New York accent*]: You mean to tell me he wouldn't take a nickel?
> *Second voice* [*also New York*]: Not a quawtuh. You see what he did again this week? Took out the gar-

bage, the ashes out, cleaned up the lawn. Wouldn't say nothin'. Won't take a nickel. Loves people.

First voice: Get outta here.

Second voice: I'm tellin' ya. There he goes again.

Lone Ranger: HHIIIYYYOO, SIILLVERRR!

First voice: Hey, wait a minute. Masked Man! We made a party for ya, gotta present. Masked Man? He's gone again. Has he gotta broad around here? Did you give him any money?

Second voice: I didn't give him a quawtuh.

First voice: You mean to tell me this guy, every week, cleans up the yard here, takes the ashes out, did the windows with vinegar and newspaper, and he don't want nothing?

Second voice: Nothin' — won't take a nickel.

First voice: How does he live?

Second voice: I don't know. He's just selfless — he loves people. There he goes.

First voice: Hey, Masked Man!

Lone Ranger: HHIIYYOOOO, SIILLVVERRR!

First voice: Masked Man! Wait a minute! We made a party for ya and everythin, you asshole!! I'm fed up with him, already. What does he think — what is he, kidding? He saw me with my hand out there. Look, I don't mind for myself, but he saw my mother make coffee and cake and everything. The old lady came out here, to say "Thank you," and that *schmuck* drives off in his Buick. "Hiyo, Silver." He's not a nice guy. I don't wanna hear that anymore, "He's a nice guy." He's snotty. He has no humility. He came — he saw the kids with the crepe paper costumes, he knew we were making a big party for him, and he just goes off and — he's no good, I'm tellin' ya. I'm gonna kick his ass, I'm tellin' ya. Al, bring him back here. I'm gonna kick his ass all over the lot, right now. I'm tired of this horseshit, he's gonna get his ass kicked right now!

Al [*deep Southern accent*]: Hold the gun on 'im, Ma. Oh boy, my brother's hoppin'-ass mad, buddy. Phew! Our mama made all them Heyetalian cakes, you runned off. You runned off and never did say "Thank you" or nothin'. You saw him out there. What the hell, you know he get crazy like that. She came out here with coffee and cake and you ride off. How come you so good, you cain't accept nothin' from nobody? Who the hell do you think you are?

Lone Ranger: I'll explain, if you get your god-damned hands off me. (Steady, big fellow!) The reason I never wait for "Thank you" . . . supposing once I did wait for "Thank you," and I liked it. And I stuck around and I said, "Let's hear it once again."

"Hey we're in trouble. Get the Lone Ranger, get the Masked Man!"

"Just a minute. I'm getting a few 'thank-you's,' if you don't mind."

I'm gonna put my "thank-you's" in a book — a "Thank You, Masked Man" book. When I'm old, people will say, "What have you done? You haven't been in shingles all your life." No, siding business, look at this: "Thank you, Masked Man, Leo Carillo, Freeport, Long Island." I've had a good life.

And one day, someone will say, "There are no more 'thank-you-Masked-Mans' — the Messiah has returned. You see, men like yourself and Lenny Bruce, you thrive upon the continuance of segregation, violence, and disease. Now that all is pure, you're in the shit-house."

"Well, then, I'll make trouble. Because I must have a 'thank-you-Masked-Man.'"

This way, what I don't have, I don't miss. That's why I always ride off.

Al: Hot damn, you shore can talk some shit, buddy! — I gotta headache! What in hell you talkin' 'bout? Thank you Masked Man, Leo Carillo, siding business. Look, my brotha's mad, thas all I'm tellin' ya, and all you gotta do to settle the whole thing is just accept a present, that's all. I mean, what the hell you makin' a big deal outta this for? Just take a present. I'll tell 'im you accepted the present and you said thanks. I'll write somethin' on the paper, you know — "Thank

you, Mr. DiAngelo, for the present." Anything you want;
anything on the top shelf: a doll, a whip, a carton
of Luckies — go ahead.

Lone Ranger: Anything I want?

Al: Go ahead, buddy, it's yours.

Lone Ranger: No, no Luckies. Alright, gimme that
Indian over there.

Al: Who's that? Tonto?

Lone Ranger: Yes. I want Tonto the Indian.

Al: Oh, hell, you can't have Tonto.

Lone Ranger: Bullshit, you made the deal!! That's
what I want — I want Tonta the Indian.

Al: You gonna get your Tonta. His name ain't Tonta, it's Tonto. Now you cain't have Tonto.

Lone Ranger: I want Tonto. You made the deal.
I want Tonto the Indian.

Al: What the hell you want Tonto for?

Lone Ranger: To perform an unnatural act.

Al: What?!

Lone Ranger: You heard me. To perform an unnatural act.

Al: The Masked Man's a fag! Aghhhhh! He's a
fag-man. A dang queer. That's why you got that mask
on. You got masscary under there! The Fag Man.

Lone Ranger [*wistfully*]: The Fag Man . . .

Lenny Bruce: Mandrake, Lothar — all those couples.
Lothar, uh, killed a Shriner in 1936 and kept the hat —
that was his sickness. [118]

PART II

Blacks, Jews, and

Above and beyond Lenny Bruce the phenomenon, there is Lenny Bruce the man. Which is merely to say that even after analyzing the meaning and significance of his art and the pattern of suppression that was its reward, there are still a number of unanswered but by no means trivial questions clustering around the charismatic and often enigmatic figure of Lenny Bruce. What were the sources of his values? How are we to account for his apparently unique synthesis of morality and humor? From whence did he evolve his extremely personal modes of performance? What were the raw materials on which he drew for inspiration?

These questions, and others of a similar nature, are ones with which historians are traditionally more or less at home. In the case of Bruce, however, the kind of thoroughgoing, methodical research that might provide us with answers remains yet to be done. In its absence, one is forced to rely on what Lenny called his autobiography, *How to Talk Dirty and Influence People*, plus whatever other insights can be gleaned from John Cohen's attempt at systematizing Bruce's bits in *The Essential Lenny Bruce*, as well as from those hints that Lenny himself left us scattered throughout a body of recordings and unreleased tapes documenting his performances.

Lenny Bruce

For those with an abiding interest in unraveling Lenny's sometimes tangled biography, this situation is an especially unhappy one. For instance, although *How to Talk Dirty and Influence People* does indeed commence somewhat like a conventional autobiography (at least as conventional as Lenny could make it: the opening sentence begins, "Filipinos come quick," and continues in that vein), [119] the focus and the tone gradually shift from the private to the public Bruce, starting at roughly the midpoint of the book. To some extent, this may have been due to Lenny's unwillingness to probe the anguish he experienced at the ending of his stormy marriage to Honey Harlowe:

> The bad break-up is like a long-time break-up. If you're married seven years [Lenny was married for eight], you gotta kick for two. . . . I think if you're married fifteen, eighteen years, then you get divorced, . . . you must lose your mind. . . .
> There's a certain critical area there, you been married about seven, eight years, where you really throw up for a coupla years. Really, [you] just go throw up. [120]

The shift may also have been partially due to Lenny's understandably increasing preoccupation with his legal battles. Whatever the reason, the second half of *How to Talk Dirty* tends to ignore Lenny's interior evolution in favor of extensive quotations from trial transcripts, letters from physicians, clergymen, and so on. As instructive (and uproarious) as some of these excerpts may be, they don't really offer much assistance in penetrating Lenny's personal, offstage, out-of-the-courtroom world.

There are other problems with *The Essential Lenny Bruce*. It was the decision of editor-compiler John Cohen to include only one version of each of Bruce's bits. If Lenny had been the type of performer who repeated the same routines night after night, performance after performance, Cohen's approach — which was a perfectly logical and defensible one, given the fact that he was preparing a Lenny Bruce anthology rather than a compendium of Bruce's complete works — would be eminently satisfactory for research purposes. But Lenny was rather openly scornful of comedians (a category he himself transcended) who were so bereft of imagination that they never varied their bits from one show to the next. [121] In consequence, there are differences — sometimes quite significant indeed — between his bits as Cohen has transcribed them in *The Essential Lenny Bruce* and as they are heard on Lenny's recordings; [122]   there are bits that have been issued on record in more than one version; [123] there are bits in *The Essential Lenny Bruce* that are not on any record released to date; [124] and, just to complicate matters beyond belief, there are countless private tapes of Bruce's performances that have never been transcribed, released on any record, or otherwise made accessible to Brucian scholars. Clearly, therefore, "there's much work to be done now"[125]   if we are ever to be able to assemble a complete picture of the life of Lenny Bruce.

To concede that there are obstacles in the way of a definitive biography of Lenny Bruce at this time is not, however, equivalent to maintaining that no conclusions whatsoever regarding the forces and motives that he responded to are possible. Actually, Lenny himself left an assortment of tantalizing hints strewn through his writing and oral performances; in their totality, these sometimes offhand comments can be made to yield an interpretation of Bruce that, while admittedly not definitive, has substantial plausibility.

The starting point for such an interpretation, in my opinion, is the thoroughly personal vernacular that Bruce synthesized and employed. One of the relatively minor charges lodged against him by those who are either unimpressed by or unfamiliar with his work is that his esoteric vocabulary makes Bruce difficult to understand. It is true that Lenny's lexicon is scarcely that of Middle America; it is probably also true that because of this, his humor may on occasion seem unduly arcane. But to object to his choice of terms is to chase after a red herring. Lenny's use of words, as is only befitting a man who described his vocation as "distinguishing between the *moral* differences of words and their connotations,"[126] was nothing if not extremely precise. Hence it is most reasonable to suppose that Lenny's decision to invoke a certain term or phrase in preference to another, less appropriate one, was both conscious and deliberate. Indeed, this was one of the central points at issue in Bruce's "obscenity" trial in San Francisco, which initially arose out of his use of "cocksucker" instead of, say, "male homosexual," in the course of relating how he came to be booked at a San Francisco nightclub.[127] Precensoring Bruce by insisting that he employ euphemisms or a conventional vocabulary rather than the language called for by the context of each of his bits would have immediately destroyed the basis of his art—just as recasting T.S. Eliot's *The Wasteland* or Joyce's *Ulysses* in drab scientific prose would have rendered those works aesthetically and morally worthless.

It is therefore correct to stress that Bruce's characteristic idiom was elaborated with the same care that he gave to choosing the subjects he treated; and that, in fact, there is an intimate connection between the content of what he wanted to say and the words he chose—namely, that only by using a particular term or phrase could the effect he sought be achieved. To criticize Bruce for his choice of language, as some have done, is to be guilty of both paternalism and arrogance: the critic, confronted with an unfamiliar or difficult work, presumes to dictate terms to the artist whose genius has long ago been demonstrated. In this regard, Lenny's reception by the bulk of the entertainment industry press was no different in principle than that accorded by white critics to the innovative performers (such as the late John Coltrane) who created the New Black Music: Lenny was condemned for speaking the "wrong" words; the musicians were put down for playing the "wrong" sounds.[128] This implied parallel between Lenny and the Black jazz artist is a very real and significant one — in his opinion as well as my own — and one I shall return to at length subsequently.

"Perhaps at this point," Lenny wrote early in *How to Talk Dirty and Influence People*,

> I ought to say a little something about my vocabulary. My conversation, spoken and written, is usually flavored with the jargon of the hipster, the argot of the underworld, and Yiddish.[129]

So Lenny was evidently quite aware of what words he was using and the origins from which they sprang. The question that remains, then, is: Why?

Specifically, why is all of Bruce's work permeated — a word that, at the risk of appearing to correct Lenny on Lenny, I think is more accurate than "flavored" — by "the jargon of the hipster, the argot of the underworld, and Yiddish"?

It may be helpful in attempting to gain additional understanding of Bruce's private wellsprings if we attempt to put these three sources of his vocabulary into some sort of perspective. From my own exposure (which, for what it is worth, extends back into the 1950s) to his material, I would say that of the three vernaculars Lenny mentions, Yiddish is, by a slight margin, the most prominent. Next would come what Bruce terms "the jargon of the hipster," but which might with greater precision and far less zest be described as "the language of the Black art ('jazz') musician and his (rarely her) environment." "The argot of the underworld" thus occupies a relatively distant third place, and for a rather simple reason. Lenny had no organic — that is, emotional — relationship with the underworld, but instead came into contact with it primarily because the nightclub business has traditionally been (and remains) heavily penetrated by elements from the realm of organized crime. Lenny was thus thrown into contact with gangsters,[130] and as a result he adopted some of their specialized vocabulary. Yet — and this is the crucial consideration — he invoked this vocabulary solely for the purpose of conveying his own attitudes, his own stance vis-a-vis the dominant culture.

And that stance was, to put the matter bluntly, one of virtually total rejection. Bruce, as we know from the previous survey of his social satire, was horrified, repulsed, and sickened by the wholesale immorality that he saw being condoned and even actively encouraged by Establishment political, intellectual, and religious spokesmen (and women). He utilized language as a vehicle for symbolically conveying his outrage and disgust at this situation. For what is most significant about Yiddish, the highly charged language of Black musicians, and the argot of the underworld is that each of these functions as the "mother tongue," so to speak, *for a group that is beyond the pale by the standards of the dominant culture.* Yiddish-speaking Jews (i.e., those who speak Yiddish as their daily language), the cabal of Black musicians, the menacing network of gangster chieftains and petty hoodlums, all lie outside the framework of "respectable" white Anglo-Saxon Protestant society, with its socially sanctioned hypocrisy and amorality. Bruce adopted portions of the language of these three tightly knit subcultures to signify his repudiation of the present social and ethical order. By his constant use of these vernaculars, Bruce was telling us where his sympathies did and did not lie. He was telling us, in short, that when it came to Main Street, U.S.A., he might be *in*, but was definitely not *of* it.[131]

To be convinced of the validity of this proposition about the nature of Bruce's use of Yiddish and the hip terminology of Black musicians, it is first necessary to look in some detail at his views on Jews and Jewishness, and also his relationship to the world of Afro-American improvised music ("jazz").

As with most Jews — or for that matter, most non-WASPs of any variety — Lenny was able to perceive that the rhetoric of pluralism, cultural or otherwise, was an out-and-out lie when it came to describing the reality of U.S. society. To "get anywhere," to "make it," to "be a success," to "become somebody" — all of these things demanded that one take on the speech, dress, mannerisms, even to some extent the bland lifestyle of middle-class WASPs[132] — not that even then was there any guarantee that the desired rewards would be forthcoming. Because the Jews have *schlepped* with them from Europe an extended history of maintaining a culture of their own in the midst of an alien and usually hostile majority, they, perhaps more than most other non-WASP ethnic groups, have agonized incessantly over whether the ends of assimilation to the WASP mold — material gain and upward mobility — justified the means, when the latter meant sacrificing some of the most vital and positive aspects of the Jewish tradition. (This is not to suggest that the Jews were unique in their concern about the effects of assimilation, but only that they may have been more vocal in expressing it.)

With his sensitive and introspective nature, it was hardly likely that Lenny Bruce would be immune from this characteristically Jewish preoccupation with debating the advantages to be derived from "passing" into the gentile world versus the undesirability of destroying Jewish community life and values in order to accelerate the transition into ersatz WASPdom. Hence it comes as no surprise to learn that Lenny, like so many Jews, changed his name for "professional" purposes — and, again like so many Jews, felt some shame and guilt at having done so:

"Louis. That's my name in Jewish — Louis Schneider."

"Why haven't ya got 'Louis Schneider' up on the marquee?"
"Well, 'cause it's not show business. It doesn't fit."
"No, no — I don't wanna hear that. You Jewish?"
"Yeah."
"You ashamed of it?"
"Yeah."
"Why you ashamed you're Jewish?"

Lenny's response to that one was a typically laughable mixture of the real and the surreal; but in a sense it seemed to beg, not answer, the question:

> I'm not [ashamed] any more! But it used to be a problem — until *Playboy* magazine came out. Yeah, that's right. IN . . . OUT. You just can't be that urbane bachelor and drive down the street [in] a Jag or a Lotus yelling "nigger" and "kike." It don't fit. That's what's really happened.[133]

Again and again, Lenny plumbed his own pain at trying to come to terms with being a Jew in a society that reserved all the major manifestations of its approval for those who could conform to non-Jewish patterns of appearance and behavior:

> Now a Jew, in the dictionary, is one who is descended from the ancient tribes of Judea, or one who is regarded as descended from that tribe. That's what it says in the dictionary; but you and I know what a Jew is — *One Who Killed Our Lord*. I don't know if we got much press on that in Illinois — we did this about two thousand years ago. Two thousand years of Polack kids whacking the shit out of us coming home from school. Dear, dear. And although there should be a statute of limitations for that crime, it seems that those who neither have the actions nor the gait of Christians . . . will bust us out, unrelenting dues, for another deuce [two thousand].[134]

To say that Lenny was able to derive a goodly quantity of material from his various ambivalences about Christians and Jews would be a gross understatement. At one point, for example, he went so far as to divide the world into two mutually exclusive categories, Jewish and *goyish* (non-Jewish, gentile): Anything that was hip, had style, was most likely to be categorized by Lenny as Jewish, whereas anything unimaginative, cliched, cloying, or tasteless was probably *goyish.* Thus all Black people, Italians, New Yorkers, and ex-Catholic Irish-Americans were to him "Jewish," while spam, white bread, baton twirling, Georgie Jessel, Eddie Cantor, and the *B'nai B'rith* were *goyish*— as was Butte, Montana ("If you live in Butte . . . you're going to be goyish even if you're Jewish.").[135] At the other extreme, however, Bruce could long for a more WASP-like mother:

> Fay Bainter, Andy Hardy's mother, screwed up every mother in the world. She really did, man. Dig, who can be like Fay Bainter, man? Fay Bainter was always in the kitchen sweeping with an apron [on]. And Anglo-Saxon— and my mother was sweating and Jewish and hollering, man. Why couldn't she be like Fay Bainter? . . . [T]hat's what everyone wants their mother to be.[136]

One of Lenny's most explicit discussions of his ambivalence toward Christians occurs in the course of his fanciful attempt to explain the motives behind Jack Ruby's assassination of Lee Harvey Oswald. As a psychological analysis of Ruby, Lenny's account is of dubious value; but as a projection of some of Lenny's own attitudes, the bit is conceivably more revealing than he himself was aware:[137]

> No, don't really wanna— I'd really like to tell you that, you know— I'm gonna tell Christians that. Why I can tell it to you, [is] because it's all over now. I wouldn't cop out when it was goin' on. But it *is* all over now. But up to about six, seven years ago, there was such a difference between Christians and Jews,

that—but maybe you did know. Whew, forget about it. Just a line there that was just . . . No, I don't think the Christians did know it, because only the group that's involved . . . It's like—the defense counsel knows it, because he has a narrow view, where the D.A., he's hung up with a bigger practice. So it's the thing that, the Jew is hung up with his shit, and maybe the Christian—because when the Christians say, like, "Oh, is *he* Jewish? I didn't know—I can't tell when somebody's Jewish," I always thought, "That's bullshit." But he can't. Because he never got hung up with that shit, you know. "Oh, is he Jewish?" And Jews are very hung up with that all the time.

Why Ruby did it. You see, when I was a kid I had tremendous hostility for Christians my age. The reason I had the hostility is that I had no balls for fighting—and *they* could duke. So I disliked them for it, but I admired them for it, and it was a tremendous ambivalence all the time, of admiring somebody who could do that, you know, and then disliking them for it. In the neighborhood I came from, there were a lot of Jews, so the problem wasn't a big, big problem. And my elders were not concerned with punching.

But *Ruby* came from *Texas*. And a Jew in Texas is a tailor. What went on in his mind, I'm sure, is that: "If I kill a guy that killed the *President,* the Christians'll go: 'Whew! Boy, what balls he had. We always thought the Jews were chickenshit, but look at that! A JEWISH BILLY THE KID RODE OUT OF THE WEST!'"

And the Christians'll hug him and kiss him and love him and, boy, they'll say, "Oh boy, he saved everybody."

But he didn't know it was just a fantasy—from his grandmother, telling him about the Christians who punch everybody.

Even the shot was Jewish. The way he held the gun—it was a dopey Jewish way. . . . He probably went *"nach!"* too—that means "There!" in Jewish. Like, *nach! Nach!*[138]

However reluctant they may or may not have been to abandon the leading elements of their traditional ethnic-religious culture, most Jewish professionals and intellectuals — the group into which Lenny most nearly falls — of Bruce's age resolved their tension over the "place" of Jews in U.S. society in favor of assimilation — and with a vengeance. Almost entirely seduced by the fool's-gold glitter of affluence and status mobility, these Jews, especially in the post-World War II period, hastened to lend their weight to what C. Wright Mills ridiculed as "the American celebration."[139]   Believing that U.S. society was fundamentally sound in every important respect, Bruce's generation of Jewish intellectuals seemed convinced — like Richard Amsterdam, the male protagonist of Myron Kaufman's novel, *Remember Me to God*[140] — that Jews could solve whatever problems they might encounter in the U.S. simply by out-gentiling the gentiles.

Thus the spectacle of Jewish authors and scholars rushing to form the Congress of Cultural Freedom, which, during the heyday of McCarthyism, was to lodge vigorous protests against the restrictions imposed on artists, writers, and thinkers — in the Soviet Union.[141]   The USSR was axiomatically given the status of a "totalitarian" state, wholly on a par with Nazi Germany, by the Jewish cold war ideologues. Others of that group in the 1950s, and even after, proclaimed to the world their various and timely discoveries of American exceptionalism. Inasmuch as the appearance of basic class antagonisms might suggest the possibility that the U.S. had once been — or even worse, still was — something short of Utopia, obviously all such conflicts had to be expunged from history. Jewish historians helped in the heroic task of developing a New Orthodoxy, in which conflict would be banished, presumably forever, and Consensus would be permanently enshrined in its place. Never mind the embarrassing consideration that for two-thirds of its history, white society in every section of the U.S. had remained largely dependent on the slave trade and slave labor for its economic development, and that after the demise of formal slavery, a new and no less vicious system of racist quasi-slavery was erected to put Black people "in their place." Since oppression and tyranny could only exist—according to the *a priori* logic of the cold war pundits of the period—in the Soviet Union, the forcible suppression of Black people, as well as the conflicts to which it gave rise, became an un-fact, something to be overlooked rather than something to be analyzed and accounted for.

Yielding to the same cold war imperatives, Jewish academicians in the social and natural sciences helped forge new weapons for the global struggle against the monolithic Red Menace. Some, as has been mentioned, proclaimed that it was the genius of American politics to have avoided the European experience of class struggle—or for that matter, any struggle at all. Others chimed in by pointing out that ideologies—meaning, naturally, *leftist* ideologies—were now exhausted, since the affluent U.S. had solved its outstanding social problems. Well, almost all problems—there was still the massive danger to the Republic posed by the existence of domestic communists, as Jewish publicists and writers liked to point out. Some of them therefore applauded gleefully, as was only just and proper, when those arch-traitors, Julius and Ethel Rosenberg, were apprehended, tried, convicted, and executed; while others preferred instead to concentrate on whipping up public support for a noble patriot who was being unfairly maligned, the late junior senator from Wisconsin.[142] In any case, it was clear that radicals and left-wingers were the major (if not the sole) cause of the world's woes. Modern political movements organized around anti-Jewish (mistakenly called anti-Semitic) goals, for instance, had not originated with Austrians and Germans, as so many less sophisticated laymen naively believed. On the contrary, Jewish researchers exclaimed with a triumphant flourish, anti-Jewish politics were pioneered during the 1890s in the U.S. by proto-fascistic agrarian leftists, demonstrating beyond a shadow of a doubt that all evils could ultimately be traced back to radical roots.

Meanwhile, on the international front, Jewish intellectual technicians were thinking the unthinkable about lobbing nukes into the men's room of the Kremlin; or were composing anticommunist refrains, under the guise of Non-Communist Manifestos, on the subject of economic "growth" — and then, when reality in Southeast Asia failed to conform to the anticommunist pipe dream, devised "Plan No. 6" for bombing reality into a more malleable state.[143]

Daniel Bell's observation that intellectuals "found new virtues in the United States because of [among other things] the expanding opportunities for intellectual employment" is nowhere more applicable than to the Jewish intellectuals of Lenny Bruce's age group. The remainder of Bell's comment is also worth quoting for its relevance to that group: "And, in the growing Cold War, they accepted the fact" — *fact?* — "that Soviet Russia was the principal threat to freedom in the world today."[144] One may disagree with Bell about what is and what is not a "fact," but it would be hard to improve upon the theory of causation implicit in his statement.

Regardless of the degree to which Lenny might have envied the WASPs, with their Fay Bainter mothers and their "winner chicks,"[145] regardless of how self-conscious or maybe even ashamed of his Jewishness he may sometimes have been, it was a foregone conclusion that he would not — indeed, could not — ape the bulk of the Jewish educated classes in their mindless scramble after the supposed goodies of the affluent society. I say this not because Lenny lacked the ability to "pass." Quite the contrary. His work preserved on tape and record reveals that Lenny was an incredibly gifted, even brilliant, mimic. In one and the same bit, he could take on in rapid succession three or four different characters, each with a distinct voice and accent pattern, render each part with absolute fidelity, and never once get the characters confused.[146] He also had a flair for picking up snatches of other languages with amazing rapidity; and, as one of the pictures in *How to Talk Dirty and Influence People* reveals, he could even remodel his appearance to resemble the 1940s movie-matinee concept of the suave Romeo, complete with pencil-thin mustache.[147] Certainly, if any Jew had the talents required for getting on in the gentile world, Lenny was the one.

Yet while Lenny might prune all the Yiddish words

out of his vocabulary, alter his speech so as not to have
a recognizably Jewish inflection, recast his appearance
so as not to "look Jewish," and so on, the one thing he
could *not* do was to extirpate his Jewish conscience.
This is where Lenny differed most markedly from many
of his formally educated Jewish peers, who apparently
found it not too difficult to slough off the religious teachings of their childhood if such teachings encumbered them
on the path to social advancement. Unlike them, Lenny
was blessed (or cursed, depending on one's point of
view) with the kind of abiding moral sense that made
it impossible for him to still his conscience in the name
of expediency.

To see this, one need look no further than the Rosenberg case. The American Congress for Cultural Freedom,
as pointed out earlier, was led largely by Jews; its position vis-a-vis the Rosenbergs accurately reflects the desire of Jewish intellectuals of that period to demonstrate
their superior civic-mindedness and patriotism, which in
this instance meant little more than establishing their
credentials as rabid haters of "communism" and "communists." Jewish intellectuals therefore tended to perceive the
Rosenbergs — who were, of course, ethnically (if not re-
ligiously) Jewish — as an enormous embarrassment which
might, however, with assiduous effort, be turned into a
stroke of good fortune. Leslie Fiedler, for one, a Jew who
contributed frequently to *Encounter*, the magazine published with Central Intelligence Agency funds through
the Congress for Cultural Freedom, thus lost no opportunity to proclaim his faith in — the Rosenbergs' guilt.
"To believe that two innocents had been falsely condemned"
to death, Fiedler snorted, "one would have to believe the
judges and public officials of the United States to be
not merely the Fascists the Rosenbergs called them, but
monsters, insensate beasts."[148] Which is, of course, just
what a few hardy souls (including, to their credit, some
Jews), who refused to be cowed by the all-pervasive
Red Scare atmosphere of the period, continued to maintain throughout. Moreover, having seen some of these
"judges and public officials" connive in the persecution of
Lenny Bruce — to say nothing of the repression of the

Black Panthers, the Berrigan brothers, and the Chicago Eight, or the annihilation of entire populations in Southeast Asia with the most barbarous warmaking methods imaginable—having seen these people in action, the description of them as "monsters, insensate beasts" does not seem unduly harsh.

The same callous disregard for humane values and the same willingness to subordinate every other consideration to that of anticommunist expediency is also apparent in the CCF's directive setting forth the permissible manner in which its members might involve themselves in the Rosenberg case:

> The pre-eminent fact of the Rosenbergs' guilt must be openly acknowledged before any appeal for clemency can be regarded as having been made in good faith. Those who allow the Communists to make use of their name in such a way as to permit any doubt to arise about the Rosenbergs' guilt are doing a grave disservice to the cause of justice—and of mercy too. [149]

As if the CCF leadership gave a plugged nickel for mercy!

It is instructive to compare the response to the Rosenberg case of the CCF, whose policies were largely shaped by middle-class, respectability-seeking Jewish "intellectuals," with that of Lenny Bruce:

> Goddamn the priests and the rabbis. Goddamn the Popes and all their hypocrisy. Goddamn Israel and its bond drives. What influence did they exert to save the lives of the Rosenbergs—*guilty or not?* [Emphasis added.] Again, the Ten Commandments doesn't say "Thou Shalt Not Kill *Sometimes* . . ." [150]

The issues raised by the Rosenbergs dramatically illustrate the unbridgeable gulf that had opened up between Lenny and the bulk of the Jewish professionals and intellectual technicians of the same generation. To Lenny, the saving of a human life—whether capitalist, communist, anticommunist, or whatever — always took priority. To his fellow Jews, however, the main consideration was not that of saving the lives of the Rosenbergs, but saving face in the eyes of the gentiles. In practice, this seemingly dictated that Jewish writers, academicians, and cold warriors generally demonstrate their "loyalty" by being harsher on the Rosenbergs — witness Leslie Fiedler and the CCF — than their non-Jewish counterparts.

In turning their backs on the Rosenbergs, the Jewish intellectuals were not just abandoning two forlorn people to the ideological exigencies of the cold war and the (nonexistent) mercies of the state. More than that, they were also abandoning a central and immensely important aspect of Jewish tradition. This emerges readily if we simply look at the definition of a Yiddish word, *rachmones*, that Lenny loved to invoke. (With *emmis*, truth, it was one of his favorites.) "This quintessential word," writes Leo Rosten of *rachmones*,

> lies at the heart of Jewish thought and feeling. All of Judaism's philosophy, ethics, ethos, learning, education, hierarchy of values, are saturated with a sense of, and heightened sensitivity to, *rachmones*.
>
> God is often called the God of Mercy and Compassion: *Adonai El Rachum Ve-Chanum.*
>
> The writings of the prophets are permeated with appeals for *rachmones,* a divine attribute. . . .
>
> Note that the Hebrew root *rechem,* from which *rachmones* is derived, means "a mother's womb." *The rabbis taught that a Jew should look upon others with the same love and feeling that a mother feels for the issue of her womb* [emphasis added]. "He is in such straits one can only have *rachmones* on him." "The least one can show is *rachmones.*"

Hence the Rosenberg case crystallized in microcosm the entire dilemma of the Jewish intellectuals in the postwar period: to adhere to time-honored values at the risk of foregoing the material and other dividends of superconformity to WASP norms, or to repudiate those values that interfered with the pursuit of wealth and status. Lenny

Bruce, as we have seen, ultimately took the first road; his Jewish contemporaries among the intellectuals chose the latter. [151]

Some Jewish intellectuals of Bruce's generation, to be sure, did maintain a nominal, perfunctory synagogue attendance, sometimes combined with a kind of *pro forma* observation of Jewish ritual in the home; while others have become ardent Zionists. All of these essentially private gestures, however, have not substantially impeded the flight from Jewish life and values. If anything, in fact, they may have even served to accelerate it, by helping Jews to deceive themselves that such largely empty and meaningless measures would somehow suffice to preserve the significant aspects of the tradition intact. What triumphs in the long run, however, is not form but content; and the content of life for most Jewish intellectuals has been increasingly non-Jewish in matters of morals and values. [152]

On this point, too, Lenny was in disagreement with the socially mobile intellectuals. Without in the least denying that being a Jew sometimes produced ambivalence in him, the fact of the matter is that Lenny seems never to have entertained the notion of allowing himself to be publicly identified as anything *but* a Jew; and he scarcely bothered to disguise his contempt for those who, in one way or another, attempted to minimize their Jewishness when among gentiles. Hence although he was too much the rationalist and skeptical anticleric ever to belong to *any* formal religious denomination, [153] it is both clear and significant that he reserved most of his criticism of organized Jewry for the hyperassimilationist and quasi-Protestant Reform Jews and their rabbis. Virtually every time he even mentioned a Reform *shule* (temple) or a Reform rabbi, he would follow it with the words: "so Reform they're ashamed they're Jewish." [154] The rather transparent intellectual dishonesty involved in altering Jewish rituals so as to reassure the assimilationist-minded that they were not really very different, after all, from their Protestant colleagues, did not much appeal to Lenny. Thus whenever he chose to satirize a Jewish religious leader, as in "Religions, Inc.," he would invariably choose a Reform rabbi, usually Stephen S. Wise, to join Oral Roberts, O.L. Jaggers, Billy Graham, Patamunzo Yoganunda, Eddie Cantor, and Pat O'Brien (as the priest) as objects of his humor. [155] Bruce was evidently quite shocked to discover just how far Protestantizing tendencies had gone on the West Coast, and if he wanted to lampoon some especially gross absurdities perpetrated under the rubric of Reform Judaism, he pointed to the Reform *shules* he encountered there for illustrations (as in this excerpt from one version of "Christ and Moses"):

> I bet you, when Christ and Moses return, the *shules* have had it first.
> Saturday they would make every kind of *shule* — a drive-in *shule,* Frank Lloyd Wright *shule,* West Coast *shule.* . . . Santa Monica [California] — there is that A-frame *shule* that they just put the statues in:
> "Are you putting a *madonna* in the *shule*?"
> "Yes, it's contemporary, that's all."
> "*Whew!* Don't figure out, man . . . uh, [are] they *supposed* to have one?"
> Yes, there is a Reform temple where the rabbi — no, it's a doctor, he is a doctor of law. His beard is gone, because he was called a beatnik. And now he has this sound:
> "You know, someone had the *chutzpah* [nerve] to ask me the other day — they said, 'Tell me something, Doctor of Law, is there a God or not?' What cheek, to ask this in a temple! We're not here to talk of God — we're here to sell bonds for Israel! Remember that! A pox upon you, Christ and Moses!" [156]

Bruce's constant employment of Yiddish — to return to that subject after somewhat of a digression — also has to be understood in the same context as another indication of his opposition to the assimilationist impulses of the educated, middle-class Jews of his generation, and to the cruelly cutthroat society into which they sought to merge. On the most obvious level, Lenny's use of Yiddish words and phrases, particularly some of the less well-known ones, amounted to his manifesto of Jewishness, announcing his refusal to be perceived in public as anything but a Jew. More significantly, however, by continually incorporating Yiddish into his performances, Lenny was attempting to invert the logic of the assimilationists. For the latter, their Jewishness was, if not something to be concealed, certainly a topic to be disposed of as rapidly and antiseptically as possible. Accordingly, assimilationist Jews ruthlessly pruned themselves of any habits of speech, gestures, or other forms of behavior that might seem congruent with prevailing Jewish stereotypes (of which they, as Jews, were probably far more aware than most of their non-Jewish associates). 157 Needless to say, such assimilation-bound Jews would rather die (already) than have a word or two of Yiddish accidentally slip out in the company of gentile colleagues.

Lenny, on the other hand, took a diametrically opposite tack. *His* assumption was not that he, as a Jew, should learn to conform to the expectations and mores of the gentiles, but rather that the gentiles should be exposed to some of the time-honored ethical values of Jewish life and thought—*rachmones* being an excellent case in point—and that *they* should assimilate *that.* This set Lenny even further apart from contemporary Jewish comedians, such as Joey Bishop, Mort Sahl, Phyllis Diller and Shelley Berman, who tacitly accepted the premises of the assimilationists by working entirely in English. (It also distinguished him from those Jewish comics like Mickey Katz who worked largely in Yiddish but to almost exclusively Jewish audiences.) Here again, Bruce's daring and vision as an innovator emerge, for no one else had either the audacity or the imagination to presume that Jewish intellectuals, rather than attempting to become soulless copies of their gentile counterparts at the cost of their unique and humanistic morality, should instead seek to humanize the gentiles by giving them an extended exposure to the best qualities in the Jewish heritage. It is scarcely necessary to add that Bruce's approach to the question of assimilation, which postulated bringing non-Jews into *his* unmistakably Jewish world rather than the reverse, was a standing rebuff to the status strivings of assimilationist-minded educated Jews, as well as another form of his rejection of an unjust and oppressive WASP-dominated status quo.

But Bruce's relationship to Judaism extended beyond simply using Yiddish as a symbolic weapon in his battle against assimilationist ideas. As the final point in this discussion of Lenny's relationship to Judaism, therefore, I would like to suggest that he drew upon—or better yet, embodied—several important strands from the fabric of Jewish tradition. To begin with, Lenny combined the functions of a number of different types of holy persons found in Orthodox Jewish communities—and it was precisely among such Orthodox Jews (e.g., his Aunt Mema) that he was raised. Taking the various holy men in order, there is:

1. *The Rabbi.* The Hebrew word from which rabbi is derived, *rebbe,* has the literal meaning "teacher"—a function Lenny fulfilled supremely well. The early rabbis, it should be realized, were "not professional clergymen at all"—the transition from rabbi to "Jewish priest" was another product of assimilationist thinking—but were rather, according to Leo Rosten, "men superior in character, probity, learning, whom the community respected. They exercised moral leadership, acted as judges, counselors, exemplars of conduct."[158] Rosten also writes:

> The title "rabbi" does not have the same connotation as does "priest" or "minister." A rabbi is not an intermediary between God and man, as is, say, a Catholic priest. . . . His position traditionally gives him no power, no hierarchical status. . . .
> Down the centuries, the sages stressed that scholars must share their knowledge with the less learned, *and their insights with the less spiritually sensitive; hence rabbis were enjoined to spread instruction and enlightenment, to uplift the moral, ethical and religious life of their congregations. . . .*[159]

So, ironic as it may seem—and as much as it might shock Lenny himself—there is a good prima facie case to be made for considering Bruce a functioning rabbi in secular drag (to use his own lexicon).

2. *The Maggid.* Rosten's definition of the *maggid* is: "A teacher-preacher, usually itinerant." *Maggidim* (plural of *maggid*) developed as rabbis increasingly devoted themselves to the scholarly study of the law, thus becoming aloof "from the pains and problems of ordinary people." Into this void stepped the *maggid:*

> A humble, often untidy, shabbily clothed "country preacher," he wandered about on foot, by cart, by wagon, from *shtetl* to *shtetl* [town to town] — teaching, preaching, comforting, *an evangelist concerned with the poorest among the tribe of Israel.*

The last clause, of course, offers us another fitting description of Bruce — except that he didn't limit his ministrations to Israelites. And Lenny also matches Rosten's account of the *maggid* in several other respects as well: his use of the vernacular to express blunt home truths (whereas rabbis, as scholars, employed the more high-flown Hebrew); and his general approach to his followers (or congregation):

> . . . [T]he most beloved *maggidim* were the homey-philosopher types — good-natured, *humane, tolerant of human frailty, skillful in mixing jokes, stories and parables into their sermons.*[160]

Doesn't that sound like Lenny? "Humane, tolerant of human frailty" — enough so as to be able to *hab rachmones* for the white Southerner, even the hapless Ku Kluxer. "Skillful in mixing jokes, stories and parables into [his] sermons." Was anyone *more* skillful than he? Remember "The Masked Man"? "Christ and Moses"? "The Tribunal"?

3. *The Tzaddik.* The literal translation is "a most righteous man." *Tzaddikim* were believed to be men — apparently women could not qualify among traditional Jews, who were strongly male-chauvinist in most religious matters (e.g., women were not taught Hebrew, the language of talmudic scholarship, but were instead confined to speaking Yiddish) — doing good works in secret and vanishing immediately thereafter. Rosten observes with regard to the *tzaddikim* that

the idea of doing good secretly, without reward, fleeing from any recognition or gratitude, held great fascination for the men of the *Talmud.* The less publicly a good deed is done, the more for its own quintessential goodness, the more admirable it is. Heaven will know . . . God will remember. [161]

And there, obviously, is the source for Lenny's "Lone Ranger/Masked Man" fantasy. Lenny himself, as that bit implied, had a strong streak of the *tzaddik'*s traditional humility about him:

All my humor is based upon destruction and despair. If the whole world were tranquil, without disease and violence, I'd be standing on the breadline right in back of J. Edgar Hoover and . . . Dr. Jonas Salk. [162]

If it seems ludicrous to propose that Lenny Bruce, ostensibly just a nightclub comic, synthesized elements of the rabbi, the *maggid*, and the *tzaddik,* the ludicrousness — to paraphrase Lenny on the obscenity of toilets — is in the eye of the beholder. In reality, the combination of spiritual leader — which I suspect is as close as we may ever get to putting a name on Lenny's vocation — and comedian makes eminently good sense from the standpoint of Jewish tradition. First of all, the comic is himself (or herself) a recurrent figure in Jewish tradition; having been entertained by Jewish humor from Jack Benny and the Marx Brothers to Lenny Bruce and his contemporaries, we should not require further elaboration. [163] Secondly, Jewish tradition does not confine its holy persons and religious figures to places of worship. Rather, as the quotations from Rosten have already indicated, both the *maggidim* and the *tzaddikim* were expected to mingle with the masses, wherever they were to be found. Even the rabbis themselves, for that matter, were originally humble artisans and laborers. Hence there is no contradiction whatsoever involved in "preaching" from the stage of a nightclub or theater. If that is where people can be reached — why not? [164]

Finally, humor itself has an important position in the

transmission of Jewish tradition, particularly that portion dealing with ethical relations among people. Leo
Rosten, in *The Joys of Yiddish,* puts the point cogently
when he writes that he considers

> the story, the anecdote, the joke, a teaching instrument
> of unique efficacy. A joke is a structured, compact
> narrative that makes a point with power, generally
> by surprise.[165] A good story is exceedingly hard for
> anyone to forget. It is therefore an excellent pedagogic
> peg on which to hang a point. . . .
>   [Moreover, the] Jewish anecdote possesses a bou-
> quet all its own. Since almost every Jew is raised
> to reverence learning, and is encouraged to be a bit
> of a teacher, the Jewish story (*myseh*) is at its best
> when it points a problem or moralizes a problem.[166]

If that be the case, then it should not take much of a
leap for us to realize that Lenny was the incarnation of
all that is the best—in *every* sense of the word—in a
long, potent, extremely humanistic and, not least, very
funny tradition of Jewish humor.

Is it merely coincidence that the first two sections of
The Essential Lenny Bruce deal with Jews and Blacks?
Perhaps; but if so, the coincidence is an extremely pro-
vocative one.

In the previous passages I sought to demonstrate the
proposition that Lenny Bruce invoked several aspects
of the Jewish tradition, the Yiddish vernacular promi-
nently among them, as a two-edged sword: first, to symbolize his rejection of a WASP-controlled society that he
considered lacking in honesty, decency, mercy, and
morality; second, to symbolize his identification with the
most valuable ethical concepts that he learned as part
of his Jewish heritage. To that proposition I would now
add that essentially the same thesis can be advanced
with respect to Lenny's debt to Black culture, especially
that of the improvising Black (jazz) musician. Since, as
you may have noticed, Lenny was neither genetically
Black—though he became, in my opinion, *culturally*

Black—nor a practicing musician, this latter thesis will also require some defense if it is to be accepted.

It is genuinely unfortunate that white scholars of social and intellectual history in the universities have thus far almost completely neglected Black culture in general — and that of the improvising Black musician in particular — as an exceptionally fertile source of new developments in the culture of this country (the most fertile source of any, in my opinion). To take one humble but representative example, most of the argot terms used today by young people in the counter-culture have their origins in Black musicians' circles; several of them, indeed, date back as far as four or more decades. Apparently, however, this realization has not gained general currency, and many students of the counter-culture — even many of the participants themselves, for that matter — actually believe that young white cultural dissidents, rather than Black musicians, have invented such terms as "groovy," "far out," "hip," "jam" (as in "jam session"), (to be) "into" (something), his (her, your or my) "own thing," "bread," "wow" (as in: "Oh, wow!"), "threads," "funky," "joint" (for either prison or marijuana cigarette), "grass," "pot," "weed," and "smoke dope," "get down," "busted," "freak" (or "freak out"), "killer" (i.e., very good), "to burn" (i.e., cheat or swindle), "head" (as a noun or noun suffix, e.g., "pothead"), "out-of-sight," "mellow," and so forth.[167]

The point is worth making explicitly simply because the rhetoric of Lenny Bruce is replete with expressions drawn from this source, but — given the pervasive ignorance about Black culture, its myriad aspects and the innumerable "borrowings" of its styles and products by whites — his use of terms from the Black music milieu is quite likely to go unrecognized. Without even attempting to specify the precise locus of each and every one of them, it is still the case that Lenny was *constantly* incorporating such words and phrases as "get next to" (become friendly or intimate with), "twisted" (insane or obsessed), "have eyes for" (to like or to want a person or thing), "be cool," "dig," "cat" (for male), "Jim" or "man" (salutations popular among musicians: "It's that cold, Jim"),[168] "gig" (job), "make it with" (have sexual relations with), "pay some

dues" (suffer for), "bugged" (with or by), and countless others, into all of his routines. So much so, in fact,
that Orrin Keepnews, who has been a producer of jazz
records for nearly a quarter century, recalled shortly
after Lenny's death that speaking with him "was *so* much
like conversation with a jazz musician that it was hard
to remember that I wasn't talking with one." Keepnews
goes on to add: "I can think of no other non-musician
about whom I can make that statement."[169] Coming from
a man with such extensive experience with Black musicians, his testimony carries considerable weight.

Lenny himself, of course, obliquely acknowledged his
persistent reliance on the Black musician's vernacular when
he wrote that his "conversation, spoken and written, is
usually flavored with the jargon of the hipster. . . ."[170]
In actuality, however, his relationship to the world of
Black music went quite a bit deeper, as Lenny explicitly recognized, than simply the use of the "jargon of the
hipster" for "flavoring" his work. As was the case with
his recourse to Yiddish, Lenny drew on Black music
sources for some of his concepts about both form and
content, technique and substance.

It isn't clear from his autobiography when or where
Lenny's initial encounter with Black music occurred, but
probably his most extended single exposure to the values
and attitudes of this milieu came during a four-year period in the mid-1950s while he was working steadily
in burlesque clubs in Southern California. On the gig with
him were mostly young jazz musicians of his age who,
like Lenny, found it very difficult to get jobs in so-called
"good rooms."[171]   Some of these men were Black, some
white; but the difference was not particularly crucial, since
white musicians who are seriously devoted to playing
jazz almost invariably model themselves on Black artists,
initially in matters of musical style, but subsequently in
dress, diction, cuisine, posture, as well.[172]   Lenny not
only became friendly with many of these Los Angeles
musicians—the late alto saxophonist Joe Maini was
probably Bruce's closest comrade at the time, and bassist
Leroy Vinnegar was also among his circle of in-
timates[173] —but he also fell heavily under their influence

in terms of how he conceived his own work. As a result, his style ultimately came to share many of the characteristics of improvised Black music.

The great similarity between Lenny's method of developing a particular bit and the way in which an improvising Black musician evolves a solo based on a given scale or chord progression, for example, is rather striking. As Lenny explained it:

> I've never sat down and typed out a satire. What I will do, is I will *ad lib* a line on the stage. It'll be funny. Then the next night I'll do another line, or I'll be thinking about it, like in a cab, and it'll get some form, and it'll work into a bit.
>
> Everything I do on the stage I create myself. If I do an hour show, if I'm extremely fertile, there will be about fifteen minutes of pure *ad lib*. But on an average it's about four or five minutes. But the fact that I've created it in *ad lib* seems to give it a complete feeling of free form. And the new stuff pushes the other—old—out. [174]

In much the same manner, an improvising musician who plays a solo on the same tune over a prolonged period will be continually incorporating new ideas into the basic framework of the piece and discarding concepts that have turned stale, predictable, boring. This procedure helps to preserve a certain amount of underlying continuity, while still permitting the musician to hold his (or her) own and the listener's interest by introducing new and generally more challenging material over time. [175]

Orrin Keepnews, from whose account I have already quoted, saw other similarities "between [Lenny's] technique and that of at least some jazz musicians." One of these was the inclusion in Lenny's bits of "touches that were clearly the equivalents of the brief but corny 'quotes' from another tune and the sardonic, dead-pan mockery with which a jazzman can approach a very square set of chord changes." Keepnews cites by way of illustration Lenny's version of a three-way conversation between Eisenhower,

his corrupt assistant Sherman Adams, and Richard Nixon.
At one point in the interrogation of Adams about the
bribes he had taken from Bernard Goldfine, Eisenhower
turns to his assistant and exclaims in a pseudo-paternal
tone:

> *Don't lie to me!* Cause, you know, I won't hit ya
> if you tell me the truth. Tell me the truth, get it off
> your chest now. You know I hate a liar. If I found
> out *later,* then I'll, you know, rap ya around a little.

In Keepnews's view, it was this weird and unexpected
twist—something very typical of all of Lenny's work—
that prevented "Ike, Sherm, and Dick" (Bruce's name for
the bit) from degenerating into "Mort Sahl-ish political
stuff."[176]

But the close parallel between Lenny and the improvising
Black musician goes beyond his procedures and techniques
alone, to include some of the fundamental principles by
which each organized his art. Lenny himself indicated that
he recognized this to be true when, after quoting a review
that said, "All Lenny Bruce seems concerned with is making the band laugh," he perceptively added:

> That should have been my first hint of the direction
> in which I was going: abstraction. Musicians, jazz
> musicians especially, appreciate art forms that are
> *extensions* of realism, as opposed to realism in a
> representational form.[177]

Extension of reality into the bizarre, the absurd, the
surreal is indeed the mode through which Bruce's humor
operates, just as extending a chord progression or a
melody line will furnish an improvising musician with
ideas for a solo. This basic approach is probably most
evident in Lenny's parodies of movies, such as *The Defiant Ones,* where the "reality"—in this case, the film's
original plot—is usually absurd to begin with. It is less
explicit—but no less funny—in a number of other scenarios that may have originated in reality but were extended

by Brucian logic to a fantastic conclusion: Think what might happen if the Lone Ranger began waiting for "thank you's." What would we hear if we could eavesdrop on a white person attempting to entertain a Black person at a party, with Whitey too drunk to conceal his racist fears and stereotypes? Apply the marijuana-leads-to-heroin syllogism to gambling at church benefits. Suppose one were to respond to the word "cocksucker" as if it really meant just that. Imagine taking your children to a "dirty movie" instead of a violent and bloody one. Other bits utilized the same principle, but required more than just a simple, straightforward extension of reality — a leap, perhaps: What if Christ and Moses were to return to earth and visit St. Patrick's Cathedral on a Sunday? Suppose high-paid performers were put on trial and forced to justify their extravagant incomes. Think of the dismay of white liberals who consider themselves firm supporters of integration when confronted with an all-Black jury.

Although the scope of this analysis could easily be broadened to encompass most of the longer scenarios that have been issued to date on recordings, three relatively brief excerpts should serve to convey what Lenny meant when he described the basic principle behind his humor as the "*extension* of reality." The first of these is his variant on a standard — indeed, trite — gambit with which many a comedian has opened a performance:

If you've, uh, ever seen this bit before, I want you to tell me — stop me if you've seen it. [*Pause*] I'm going to piss on you. [*Laughter and applause*] So much spurious acceptance, see that? I can't take the bit out.

Every time I say — I just started it as a gag once, you know, and they just say, "Hurray, hurray!"

"Lemme just do a few talk bits first."

But, no — "Piss on us first, and then you'll do the rest of the bits."

Now, I tell you this because some of the ringsiders have objected to it. And it's just fair to warn you, that's all. I don't make any great show of it — I just do it, and that's all. [178]

The second is the final item in a bit Lenny called "Three Commercials You'll Never See on Television":

> Commercial number three.
> *First voice:* I don't know what the hell it is, Bill—I been smokin' this pot all day and I still can't get high on it.
> *Second voice:* What kind are ya smoking?
> *First voice:* Well, all marijuana's the same, isn't it?
> *Second voice:* That's the mistake a lotta people make.[179]

Last is the concluding portion of a longer (untitled) bit dealing with what Lenny felt to be differences in the nature of men and women. His argument was that women should not be hurt by male promiscuity, because men, unlike women, were allegedly eager to have sexual relations with persons whom they did not necessarily love. Whatever one may think of this proposition, it must be conceded that Lenny brings the bit to a close in his characteristically outrageous fashion:[180]

> It's a different emotion, different thing with guys. And if you came home and you found your husband, really, sitting on the bed with a chick or a *chicken*—you really shouldn't feel that you were betrayed. Really. Or wanna leave 'im, or be that hurt and cry.
> *Wife:* A chicken! Don't talk to me. In our bed—a chicken. No, I'm not angry, but leave me alone, that's all. You want dinner, get your chicken to get it for you.
> How come you came home early tonight? Your chicken left town, eh? Go out with your chicken, have a good time. Don't need me. Go out with your fancy chicken.
> *Husband:* I don't want any chicken. I was drunk, I met her in the yard. Whaddya want from me? I just did it to make you angry, that's all. I don't care about the chicken.[181]

Lenny may not have wished to be assimilated among the WASPs, but he was unquestionably willing to acculturate with the Blacks, especially Black musicians. Evidently the admiration was mutual, for as Orrin Keepnews makes clear, "Bruce attracted jazz people in particular" right from his first New York appearance in 1959. At that point, Lenny was in the final phase of moving from burlesque clubs to better-paying jobs, and the word-of-mouth reputation he had already developed among musicians was undoubtedly a substantial asset in ensuring that the transition was a smooth, successful one. Much of this reputation was spread single-handedly by Philly Joe Jones, the Black drummer with Miles Davis during the late 1950s who was universally acknowledged as one of the outstanding innovators on his instrument. Philly Joe's enthusiasm for Lenny took a number of forms: proselytizing for Lenny's opening engagement in New York; recording, under the title *Blues for Dracula,* his tribute to Bruce's parody of a Bela Lugosi film; and the ultimate in flattery, planning with Bruce to utilize his talents in the *sui generis* role of "talking sideman" on one of Philly Joe's own Riverside jazz albums. (This project went so far that Lenny at one point sent Orrin Keepnews, who was then half owner of Riverside, the script that he and Philly Joe were intending to use.) [182]

Philly Joe was certainly something of a zealot where Lenny Bruce was concerned; but as I've already pointed out, this was by no means an individual idiosyncrasy among Black musicians or jazz people in general. In fact, because Lenny's standing with musicians was so high, he ended up being booked into certain nightclubs that were otherwise devoted exclusively to music. Such was the case, for example, with the Jazz Workshop in San Francisco. Its owner, according to Orrin Keepnews, had known of Lenny "for a long time and had very much wanted to have him work there— . . . the only nonjazz act [the owner] ever coveted." [183]

The analysis of Lenny Bruce's relationship to the culture of Black musicians would not be complete without some indication of the way in which his prolonged exposure to that culture profoundly **affected** the content of his art, particularly his moral stance with respect to U. S. society.

Performing for several years in close proximity with improvising Black musicians (and white musicians who shared their attitudes)— a group whose genius historically has gone as grievously unrecognized as it has been ruthlessly exploited [184] —was, in my opinion, an experience of inestimable value for Lenny. We have already witnessed some of the ways in which this experience shaped his approach to humor. In addition to that, however, it also sharpened Bruce's social and ethical perceptions. In a general and largely abstract way, he was undoubtedly familiar with the oppression of Black people in U.S. society. My hunch is that, more than anything else, working side by side with immensely talented Black musicians provided Bruce with the insights necessary to make these abstractions take on visceral, flesh-and-blood meaning.

If the foregoing reasoning is correct, then it would be difficult to conceive of anything that could have had a more beneficial effect on Lenny's development as a social thinker and satirist than his experiences performing with Black musicians. (It is surely significant in this context that the only person known to me who ever performed onstage with Bruce after 1960 or thereabouts was Black guitarist Eric Miller.) *For what these experiences did was to give Bruce a sustained opportunity to work out and apply in practical terms those traditional precepts that he had absorbed from the teachings of Judaism.* The Jewish ethical-cultural heritage that he had been imbued with as a youth, such as the unremitting emphasis on every decent person's obligation to *hab rachmones* for others who were less fortunate, could thus be revitalized and synthesized with the contemporary plight of the politically downtrodden and economically deprived Black people. Moreover, the heavy stress in Jewish history on resistance to oppression could only facilitate the process of bringing Jewish ethical and social values to bear on the Black movement for human rights.

If there is any single circumstance that propelled Lenny's most mature work to its highest point of fruition, it would be, in my estimate, the conjunction of Jewish values and

Black suffering that occurred when Bruce entered the world of Black musicians. I do not believe that the significance of this conjunction can be exaggerated, for his concern for Black people—like his use of Black musicians' vernacular and his own Yiddish—permeates his work, and to a greater degree than any other subject. Indeed, it is difficult to think of a major Lenny Bruce bit that does not have at least one reference—whether veiled, oblique, implied, or direct—to Black people and their harsh lot in a racist society. Several of his best-known recorded bits, of course, are devoted explicitly to this topic: on *"I Am Not a Nut, Elect Me!"*, *"The Defiant Ones"* and "Our Governors"; on *Lenny Bruce—American*, "How to Relax Your Colored Friends at Parties"; on *To Is a Preposition and Come Is a Verb*, "A White, White Woman and a Black, Black Woman"; on *The Essential Lenny Bruce: Politics*, "Black Democracy and Liberals." (Two of his records, *The Midnight Concert* and *Lenny Bruce Is Out Again*, are not divided into individual tracks and hence cannot be included in this survey.)

But what is more impressive still is the number of bits that deal with ostensibly non-racial topics, and yet suddenly and abruptly shift to focus on racism and the oppression of Black people as a means of making a point.

In "Father Flotski's Triumph,"[185] for instance, a bit to be analyzed in greater detail presently, a Death Row scene is employed as a vehicle to satirize white stereotypes about Black people, much as in "How to Relax Your Colored Friends at Parties." In "Religions, Inc.," Bruce seizes upon the fact that religious spokesmen sanction segregation (Oral Roberts to the pope: "Naw, I dunno what the hell *they* wanna go to school for, either!") as a dramatic means of underlining the institutionalized hypocrisy of the organized denominations on clear-cut moral issues; and he employs much the same technique on "Christ and Moses" (Cardinal Spellman to the pope, speaking of Christ and Moses: "Of course they're white!").[186] Lenny again brings up segregation in passing (so to speak), as if to castigate the society whose official leaders are willing to condone it, in the course of describing "My Trip to Miami."[187] Likewise, among his arguments for

refusing to support Radio Free Europe or the notion
of "freeing" people from communism was the fact that
the U. S. itself was not free for Black people. [188] And
this list could readily be extended.

In this context, it is also appropriate to call attention to
the cover of what I consider to be one of Lenny's most
brilliant recordings, "*I Am Not a Nut— Elect Me!*" In the
background is a statue of Abraham Lincoln seated; directly in front of that, grouped in a quarter circle, are five
figures hooded and robed in Ku Klux Klan garb — with
Black hands extending from the robes! Immediately in
front of the Black KKK contingent stands a trio comprised
of Lenny, an attractive Black woman on his right, and an
equally attractive Asian woman on his left. The placard
that Lenny holds chest-high in front of this polyglot assem-
bly reads: "TOGETHERNESS."

As another, and final, index of the thoroughness with
which Lenny digested Black-oriented values, note that at
one point he estimated his audiences to be 30 percent Black
— an amazing feat for a white performer, working for the
most part in nightclubs frequented primarily by whites.[189]
Moreover, although Lenny became diverted, and then obsessed, by his legal battles at about the time the Black lib-
eration movement began the transition from its civil rights
phase to a Black Power phase, it is not too much to suggest that Lenny would have ridden out the transition effort-
lessly, gracefully, and with his customary ability to *hab
rachmones.* Lest you doubt it, consider the following:

. . . [H]ow the world looks at the Negro — here's how
the world looks at the American Negro: he's a convict
rioting in a corrupt prison, and if they do kill Pat
O'Brien, so what? They're rioting for something they
were promised. . . .[190]

From the foregoing, it ought to be readily apparent that
Lenny developed an incredibly acute sensitivity to Black
feelings and aspirations as a result of his lengthy apprenticeship in the same milieu that Black musicians occu-
pied. This sensitivity, combined with his unfailing willingness to tell it like it is, was the touchstone for his attitudes

toward U. S. society. The colossal hypocrisy involved in
having the Establishment promote anticommunist "freedom" abroad while continuing to tolerate unfreedom for
Black people here, together with the equally obnoxious hypocrisy that Lenny perceived in the areas of sexual conduct
and organized religion, was sufficient to alienate him al-
together from the status quo. As with his use of Yiddish,
he thus invoked the idiom of the Black musician both to
show where his sympathies resided and to symbolize his
repudiation of such an obviously amoral and spiritually
diseased social system.

That being the case, I believe it a fitting gesture to bring
this effort at analyzing the roots of Lenny Bruce's ethical
values to a close with his masterful burlesque of the cliche-
ridden prison-break movie, "Father Flotski's Triumph."
I have several reasons for this choice, not least among
them the fact that Lenny — and how like him this was! —
had abiding and genuine compassion for society's most
forgotten and ostracized individuals, prison inmates, at
a time when liberal reformers (to say nothing of others)
were scarcely even aware of the existence of prisons. [191]
More germane in this context are two other facets of the
bit: first, its ridicule of the most obnoxious (and therefore
most ubiquitous) anti-Black stereotypes *and* the way Hollywood movies have helped perpetuate them; second, and
more important, the way it reveals the powerful similarity
between Bruce's approach to satire and the improvising
Black musician's approach to his art. (This point is analyzed by Orrin Keepnews in an article in *Down Beat* quoted
below.) In short, "Father Flotski's Triumph" displays in
microcosm the most prominent sources — his Jewish ethical
training synthesized with his absorption of both Black techniques and sympathies — from which Lenny Bruce drew his
inspiration.

A couple of preliminary comments. As with *The Defiant Ones,* an absolutely inane movie provides Bruce with
a remarkably effective vehicle for his satire. And although
the bit works exceedingly well as satire alone, it is probable that, as with most of his work, Bruce sought to
function here as a rabbi, a teacher — and hence there is
a serious undercurrent to be found flowing beneath the

surface of the laughter. As I have mentioned, Bruce was painfully concerned about the erosion of humanity that takes place in prison—as usual, reserving his humor for precisely those topics that he cared about most. He knew enough about prison life to be aware of the callous ways in which officials systematically manipulate religion, homosexual relationships, racial tensions, etc., as means of social control over the inmate population—even sacrificing the lives of guards and prisoners alike to the same end. All of this is present in this bit, and I believe Bruce's point will have been missed if the humor is allowed to obscure the tragedy implicit in his statement.

Lenny's "complex takeoff on a super-hackneyed prison movie called *Brute Force,*" writes Orrin Keepnews in his interpretive essay, ranks among "the best [examples] of his jazz-like technique. The trite movie itself equals a trite standard tune. The normal improvised chorus (perhaps including the soloist's own favorite cliches) would be the equivalent of some straight comedy bits in this Bruce routine—like a recurring catch-phrase yelled by the leader of the convict riot ('Ya-ta, ya-ta, ya-ta, Warden')." And now consider

the prison picture. With Charles Bickford, Barton Maclane, George E. Stone, Frankie Darrow, Warren Hymer, Nat Pendleton, and the woman across the bay, Anne Dvorak—and her two hooker friends, Iris Adrian and Glenda Farrell.

Cut to the tower, the warden—Hume Cronyn.

Prison warden [*harsh, heavy voice, heard over the loudspeaker*]*:* Alright, Dutch — this is the warden. You've got eighteen men down there, prison guards who've served me faithfully. Give up and we will meet any reasonable demands you men want—except the vibrators. Forget it, you're not getting them! Dutch! Can you hear me? This is your warden.

Dutch: Yatta-yatta! Yatta-yattayattayattah, Warden!

Warden: Never mind those Louis Armstrong impressions. Give up! You're a rotten, vicious criminal, a menace to society.

Bruce: Now the handsome but mixed-up prison doctor—H. B. Warner.

Doctor: Oh, my son . . . my son, . . . many years ago, when I knew your father, ehhh . . .

Warden: Will you come off that Billy Daniels jazz, you nitwit! Shut up, I'm the warden here—I don't want to kill anybody. Dutch, you punk, you're pushing me too far—you better give up.

Dutch: Yatta-yatta!

Warden: Shut up, you goddamned nut, you! "Yatta-yatta"—I'm sorry I gave him that library card, now. I don't know what the hell to do. Maybe if we just— maybe if we just kill a few for an example . . . that may do it! [*Over the loudspeaker*] Tower C—wanna put the cards down for a minute, huh, hm hm hm? That's right. Kill about seven hundred, down there. Go ahead! I said it's all right—now kill 'em! Come on, don't get snotty, you guys! You gonna kill 'em, now? The ones in the gray shirts. [*Pause*] The bullets? Look in the back of my brown slacks.

Forget it. Cockamamie prison, here. No one wants to help ya—I'll just . . . hm, I'll kill about sixty with my police special. 192

Keepnews continues, "But the next chorus is more daring; maybe it mocks the limitations of the syrupy tune by playing the ballad double-time, which is what happens when the stereotyped prison chaplain self-righteously elects to face the [rioting] men unarmed. . . ."

Father Flotski [*with a thick brogue*]: Wait a moment! Before there's any killing . . . I'll go down there.

Warden: Not *you*, Father Flotski!

Father Flotski: Son, I'm going down there!

Warden: Will you come off the Pat O'Brien bits, now? Father, you don't understand—these guys are monsters, they're vicious criminals, they've got knives and guns.

Father Flotski: Son, you seem to forget, don't you
. . . that I've got something stronger than a gun.
Warden: You mean . . . ?
Father Flotski: That's right! Jujitsu.
Warden: Well, you're making a mistake, Father
Flotski.
Father Flotski: Son, the mistake is mine to make,
and I'm going down there.
Bruce: Cut to the worst part of the last mile—real
Uncle Tom scene—Death Row. The first cell.
Black prisoner [*sings in deep baritone*]: Hmm, wad-
duh-boy!
Well, well. Soon I gwine up ta hebben on de big
riber boat. Den when I gets up dere, I gwinna gets
me a lotta fried chicken an waddymelone. [*Sings*]
Fried chicken and waddymelone, fried chicken and
waddymelone—dat's what I gwinna get when I get
up to dat big riber boat in heben, goddamn! Yassuh,
boss. You see, you don' min' dyin', boss, if ya got
a nach'ral sense of rhythm, yock-yock-yock.
Bruce: Now the guy is going to the chair—the last
mile.
Prisoner: So long Marty. Here's my playin' cards,
kid. Here's my *mezuzah,* Wong. And there's that door!
I don't wanna go in there—I don' know what to do, I
don' know what to do!
Black prisoner: Don' siddown, massuh![193]

"Then Lenny keeps going further and further out," Keepnews says, "until he passes mockery and hits a raw and
shocking bit of twisted reality"—which is what Bruce meant
by his phrase, "*extension* of reality"—" . . . that has nothing to do with the old movie and everything to do with
the vicious facts of [the] penal system. . . ."[194]

Back to the yard, with Father Flotski.
Father Flotski: Hello, Dutch. Dutch, you don't remember Father Flotski, now, do ya son? You know,
Dutch, you know, there's an old story that . . . once
a boy goes the bad road, the good road is hard to

follow. When the good road is hard to follow, the bad
road opens, when the good road closes . . . You're
not a bad boy, Dutch. Killing six children doesn't
make anybody bad, now. You don't remember, do
ya, Dutch, that this is Arthur Shields for Swiss Colony
Wine?

Now Dutch, I told them up there in the tier that I'd
take the gun away from ya, and I'm gonna do it,
Dutch. Now come on—there he's going to give it to
me. Come on, Dutch, give me that gun, now. [*Sotto
voce*] Come on! Will you give it to me and stop making a jerk out of me, here? Give it to me—I'll give
it *back* to ya. Take the bullets out, you jerk, you,
come on. Will you give me the gun? Ah, you'll get
it—seeing how corny you can come on. [*Screams*]
Give that gun to Father Flotski, Dutch! Come on,
are you gonna make—uh, look at all these people
watchin'. Are you gonna stop this bit—the rabbi is
watching, too. Come on. You'd sell me out, huh?

Dutch: Yatta-yatta. Yatta-yatta, Father!

Father Flotski [*incredulous*]: You're right—he's a
goddamn nut! Tried to give me all that Rosicrucian
jazz, and all those other nonscheduled theologies, there.
They're no good, the lot of them. Pour it in.

Warden: You men—the prison guards. I know this
smacks of an insalubrious deed. I've got a job to do.
The pension I'm not gonna screw up. I know it's
cold, guys, but what the hell, you know what this
gig is—it's dog eat dog. You knew what the gig was
when you took it. Only hope that your old ladies
swung with Mutual of Omaha. Dutch, you've got three
seconds—three big ones. You gonna listen to anybody?

Dutch: I'mma lissenna nobody! I'm not listenin' to
nobody in this whole stinkin' prison, Warden—nobody!

Kinky [*high, "effeminate" voice, over loudspeaker*]:
Dutch, listen to me, *bubby.*

Dutch: Who is that?

Kinky: It'th Kinky, the hothpital attendant—the one
who gave you the bed baths. Give up, *bubby,* don't
screw up your good time.

Dutch: Kinky, you *nafke* [whore], you. Kinky baby, I'll give it all up for you.

Kinky: Did you hear that? Ooooh! He's giving it up for me. I feel just like Wally Simpson. I don't believe it — he's giving it all up for *me!* Did you hear that, you bitches in cell block eleven? Ooooh — my nerves! He's giving it up for me. Did you hear him, Warden?

Warden: I heard him, ya fruit.

Kinky: Watch it, Warden — don't overstep your bounds, now. Are we going to get all our demands?

Warden: Whaddya want?

Kinky: A gay bar in the west wing.

Warden [*Yiddish inflection*]: Awright — you'll get, you'll get. What else?

Kinky: I wanna be the Avon representative of the prison. [195]

Thus Lenny Bruce. What a rare privilege it was to know him.

Lenny Bruce on Record

This essay does not pretend to be a definitive account of Lenny Bruce's recorded work — as of this writing (mid-March 1973), there is too much material still unreleased to attempt that — but simply a brief overview to guide the reader who wants some idea of the contents of the dozen or so albums to be found under Bruce's name.

Bruce's earliest recordings are on the Fantasy label. Some of the material is topical in nature, and therefore a bit dated — although, as we shall see, many of Bruce's topical barbs are no less relevant to the 1970s than to the 1950s in which they originated. All of these first albums have been edited into discrete "bits," probably excerpted from numerous performances. They do not, therefore, give a totally accurate picture of the force, scope, pacing, and continuity contained in the best of Bruce's work. A few of the bits on these records, moreover, simply drag on too long for repeated listening, which is something one expects to do with a recording; tighter editing to remove stretches of relative tedium would have benefited these bits. Still, these albums will be of interest to anyone curious about how Lenny Bruce sounded when he was just beginning to become widely known.

Lenny Bruce's Interviews of Our Times (Fantasy 7001)

is not a strictly accurate title for Bruce's only studio (as opposed to on-location or "live") recording known to me. Two of the tracks, "Shorty Petterstein's Interview" and the "Interview with Dr. Sholem Stein," are the products primarily of the imagination of Henry Jacobs, formerly general manager of KPFA-KPFB, the Pacifica Radio FM station in Berkeley. "Enchanting Transylvania" illustrates Bruce's abiding interest in Count Dracula, vampires, and the like. More memorable is "The Interview," illustrating what happens when an archetypical jazz musician/hipster/heroin addict is hired to play in the band of Lawrence Welk (whose name had to be "bleeped" out on the record to forestall a lawsuit). But a complete, more complexly surrealistic, and generally funnier version of this bit is on *Lenny Bruce: "Thank You Masked Man"* (Fantasy 7017), under the title "The Sound." Similarly, "Father Flotski's Triumph" makes its debut on this album, expurgated; the unexpurgated and therefore more profound "Triumph" is on *Lenny Bruce — American* (Fantasy 7011).

The Sick Humor of Lenny Bruce (Fantasy 7003) is valuable primarily for a classic piece of Brucian wit, "Religions, Inc." "Ike, Sherm and Dick," no doubt intended by Bruce as an extension of reality — Ike sends Dick to Lebanon to divert attention from the scandal arising when his assistant, Sherman Adams, gets caught accepting Maryland (!) as a gift from "fixer" Bernard Goldfine — pales as satire, alas, beside the present-day reality of the Watergate caper, the Soviet grain caper, the milk price caper, the ITT caper, ad infinitum. Good try, Lenny!

Sick Humor also contains "Psychopathia Sexualis," Bruce's rhymed and mordant comment on the poetry-and-jazz fad of the late 1950s. Apparently a studio-recorded track, I assume that it came from the same session that produced *Interviews of Our Times.*

With *Lenny Bruce: "I Am Not A Nut, Elect Me!"* (Fantasy 7007), Bruce's recordings approach the point of being able to suggest, and to some extent convey, the performer's genius. Each bit shows Bruce at the zenith of his form, and one, "The Palladium," is definitely a tour-de-force vignette of an overly ambitious comedian who bites off more than he can chew. This book also utilizes excerpts from three bits on this album, "The Defiant Ones," "The Tribunal," and "The Steve Allen Show."

Like *"I Am Not A Nut, Elect Me!"*, *Lenny Bruce — American* (Fantasy 7011) presents us with vintage Bruce — the social critic and commentator simultaneously at his most incisive and hilarious peak. I have already cited extensively from "How to Entertain Your Colored Friends at Parties," the unexpurgated "Father Flotski's Triumph," and, rather more briefly, "[Three] Commercials." Other highly effective bits include "Marriage, Divorce, and Motels," and Bruce's remarks on ethnicity in "Lima, Ohio" and "Don's Big Dago" (the name of a sandwich shop on Melrose Avenue in Los Angeles).

Lenny Bruce: "Thank You Masked Man" (Fantasy 7017) is a varied and uneven compilation of bits taken from years as far apart as 1958 and 1963 — whole eons in the evolution of Lenny Bruce's approach to his art. As mentioned above, this album contains a complete version of "The Sound," Bruce's account of a collision between Lawrence Welk and a hip-to-the-fingertips jazz musician. It also has Bruce's depiction of "Fat Boy," a fast-drawlin', Jew-punchin' car dealer who does his own TV commercials from the showroom of his lot in the shadow of one of the ubiquitous Southern California freeways. (I have, however, heard superior renditions of this celebrated Brucian bit in various private tape collections.) Notwithstanding the album's name, there is a considerably better rendition of "Thank You, Masked Man" on . . .

. . . *Lenny Bruce Is Out Again* (Philles 4010), the album produced for Lenny by Phil Spector. The rest of the album's contents cannot be described by itemizing the bits, as it were, because there are no separate tracks on the record. In the foregoing pages I have made use of Bruce's analysis of the Ku Klux Klan and his bit that I call "A Chick or a Chicken." This is a good, representative album (as of about 1963), released by a person who felt strongly enough about Bruce to pay for his funeral — anonymously.

There are two albums by Lenny Bruce on the Douglas label, one of which could have been excellent if properly executed, the other of which, simply, is. *The Essential Lenny Bruce: Politics* (Douglas 788) is a "concept" album — that is, an album built around a series of Lenny Bruce bits all referring to the central theme of politics. In theory a brilliant idea for a Bruce record (or records), in practice *The Essential Lenny Bruce: Politics* is fundamentally marred by production techniques that are corny, contrived, amateurish, and gimmicky; a pity that so imaginative an approach had to be subverted by a producer who, instead of having enough sense to let Lenny Bruce stand on his own two feet, apparently sought to "help" him by hoking up his material with what must be among the most dreadful sound effects known to humankind. Salvageable bits that deserve better treatment than they receive here include: "Would You Sell Out Your Country?" (alias "The Hot Lead Enema" — the same bit is on Douglas's other Bruce album), "The Bomb and Political Bullshit," "Pot Will Be Legal," "Black Democracy and Liberals."

Lenny Bruce: To Is a Preposition, Come Is a Verb (Douglas 2; later reissued as *What I Was Arrested For*) is as superb as *The Essential Lenny Bruce: Politics* could have been were its production not so appallingly tasteless. In many ways it is Bruce's outstanding single-record album. Whether inadvertently or otherwise, *To Is a Preposition* is very nearly a concept album in its own right: except for "Would You Sell Out Your Country?" (making its second appearance on a Douglas record) and "A White, White Woman and a Black, Black Woman" (also on *Lenny Bruce: Carnegie Hall,* United Artists 9800), Bruce's topic throughout is the varied manifestations of sexual taboos and hypocrisies in U.S. society. It is an incredibly powerful brew, one whose effect has not been in the least weakened by time. It is also Bruce at his most sexually explicit. Three bits — "A Pretty Bizarre Show," "Dirty Toilet" and "Blah-Blah-Blah" — recount Bruce's encounter with the law and the courts as a result of using the word "cocksucker" in a San Francisco nightclub performance. "Tits and Ass" is the ultimate analysis of both the conventional rules governing "dirty" words and the main attraction in Las Vegas supper clubs. Lenny's analysis, parallel to that by Masters and Johnson, of sexual dysfunction in men, "To Come," deservedly has the status of a classic. "I Just Do It and That's All" is a beautiful throwaway that I would have preferred to see as the closing bit. But that is an exceedingly minor quibble with what otherwise comprises a very profound, moving experience. No one else could be so funny, so witty, and simultaneously so acutely devastating a social critic. A goodly helping of that unlikely combination of qualities that Bruce possessed is preserved on *To Is a Preposition*.

Outside of "The Best of . . ." collections, which I am deliberately eschewing because I consider their basic premise misleading — the best of Lenny Bruce cannot be compressed into any two sides of a record — there remain to be discussed three multi-record albums, each documenting a different "concert" appearance by Bruce.

These concert performances — so-called, one supposes, to distinguish them from Bruce's usual nightclub work — generally presented Lenny with an opportunity to raise his art to an even higher plane. In a nightclub, there are certain constraints that govern a performance; in particular, those of time. As many of the new Black musicians have been forced to learn, the business of a club is business — not art, no matter how inspired. In concrete terms, club owners and managers prefer "sets" of an hour or less, in order to promote a rapid turnover in clientele, higher receipts at the door, and higher bar receipts (drinks are usually sold in "jazz clubs" on a per-set basis). Naturally, a performer who works nightclubs regularly will be compelled by that circumstance to tailor the material to the requisite length. This means, of course, that certain avenues of exploration are foregone entirely within those confines. And even if a member of the audience can afford to stay for an additional set, moreover, the artificial intrusion of an "intermission" dictated by the profit-taking requirements of the club owner introduces so great an element of discontinuity between sets that an artist of even Bruce's caliber will in most cases be unable to transcend it completely.

In a concert situation, on the other hand, many of these negative constraints drop away. The audience is present (one hopes) to hear a favorite performer, not to get drunk on Saturday night, and not because, having nothing better to do, its members have wandered in aimlessly off the street. And here the artist him/herself calls the shots. If there is to be an intermission, it will be at the point determined by the artist—not by a club owner. If the artist wishes to include material ordinarily too lengthy, too daring, or too innovative to use in the nightclub, there is no one to say nay. It is, in short, a much more relaxed setting, and one which a performer as sensitively attuned to an audience as Bruce was can use to maximum advantage.

Of the three concert recordings of Lenny Bruce presently available, I find the most recent one the least rewarding. *Lenny Bruce: The Berkeley Concert* (Bizarre/Reprise 6329), a two-record album produced by Frank Zappa, was taped at the Berkeley Community Theater in the mid-1960s. To judge from its contents, the performance took place not too long before Bruce's death. At any rate, he is heavily preoccupied with various speculations on the legal-juridical system; these, in fact, occupy the bulk of the album. But for all his harassment by the forces of "law and order," Bruce was still far from an easy familiarity with the terminology and terrain of the legal system. Consequently, his long disquisition on the law comes across (to me) as being somewhat diffuse and unfocused. To be sure, at this concert Bruce was occasionally brilliant, as one had come to expect, and of course funny. Yet, since he was not grounding himself, as he ordinarily did, on the raw material of intimate experience, too much of the performance is abstract and lacking in immediacy. It is not, to my way of thinking, an instance of Bruce at his most creative pitch.

That cannot be said in any respect of the other two concert performances by Bruce, however. (Unfortunately for the author, both of these three-record albums were issued after the foregoing essay on Bruce had been written.) Each of these appearances dates from 1961 and each presents Bruce at the absolute pinnacle of his form (albeit from fairly dissimilar perspectives), so that anyone with an abiding interest in him will want to hear both. *Lenny Bruce: Carnegie Hall* (United Artists UAS 9800) was recorded February 4, 1961. More leisurely and reflective than the usual Bruce nightclub performance, this album shows Lenny as he was beginning the transition away from an art based on a sequence of bits toward one that allowed him the freedom to communicate with his audience in a more spontaneous and less predetermined fashion. Among the better known bits, several of which I have excerpted in this book, are those on "Communism," "Ku Klux Klan," "Las Vegas Tits and Ass" (also on *To Is a Preposition*), "The Clap," and one of his greatest and rightly most famous scenarios, "Christ and Moses." In sum, this is a treasured source for Lenny Bruce lovers. (*Lenny Bruce: Carnegie Hall* supersedes an earlier, single-record album taken from this performance, *Lenny Bruce: The Midnight Concert* [United Artists UAS 6794]. It is from the latter that I have drawn selections for use in the text, though the footnotes take cognizance of the newer release—which, as one would anticipate, is in all respects superior.)

This is likewise the case with *Lenny Bruce Live at the Curran Theater* (Fantasy 34201), recorded and edited from a three-hour-plus performance in San Francisco in November 1961. By the time of this performance, Bruce had been twice arrested—once in Philadelphia, once in San Francisco. These arrests, logically enough, riveted his attention in an immediate way on the operation of the law in the United States, on ideal concepts of equity as opposed to the actual workings of the system of "justice," and so on. For that reason, *Live at the Curran Theater* contains many fewer bits and is more intimate, discursive, and philosophical than almost any of Bruce's other albums. It is a shame that we do not have additional, equally revealing recordings for the subsequent years up until his death. But then, this is the very least of our many shames where Lenny Bruce is concerned.

notes

1. As quoted by Lenny Bruce, *How to Talk Dirty and Influence People: An Autobiography* (paper ed.; Chicago and New York: Playboy Press and Pocket Books, 1967), p. 141. Mr. Bendich was frequently one of Bruce's defense attorneys in so-called obscenity proceedings.

2. John Cohen, ed. and comp. (New York: Ballantine Books, 1967), p. 308.

3. *How to Talk Dirty,* p. vii.

4. *How to Talk Dirty,* p. 195.

5. Ibid., p. 206.

6. Ibid., p. 178; "The Irony of Lenny Bruce," *San Francisco Sunday Examiner and Chronicle: This World,* October 31, 1971, p. 30.

7. *How to Talk Dirty,* pp. 207-10.

8. *How to Talk Dirty,* pp. 224-27; "The Irony of Lenny Bruce," *San Francisco Sunday Examiner and Chronicle,* October 31, 1971 (see note 6).

9. *Essential Lenny Bruce,* p. 271.

10. *How to Talk Dirty,* p. 182; cf. *Essential Lenny Bruce,* pp. 302-04.

11. Cf. the same "bit," as Bruce called his oral essays, on "Religions, Inc.," *The Sick Humor of Lenny Bruce* (Fantasy Records 7003); and see also *How to Talk Dirty,* pp. 75, 91-92.

12. See, e.g., *Essential Lenny Bruce,* pp. 85, 280; and the recordings *Lenny Bruce: The Berkeley Concert* (Bizarre/Reprise Records 6329); "Communism," *Lenny Bruce: The Midnight Concert* (United Artists Records UAS 6794); "Competitive System and Communism," *The Essential Lenny Bruce: Politics* (Douglas Records 8).

13. In this, Lenny resembled another charismatic spokesman for opponents of the status quo who was also struck down in his prime— Malcolm X. I have discussed the "minor lapses . . . in the rhetoric" of Malcolm X during his last months in Chapter 13 of *Black Nationalism and the Revolution in Music* (New York: Pathfinder Press, 1970), p. 257. For Lenny's ideas on performance, see *Essential Lenny Bruce,* pp. 101-33, passim.

14. See, e.g., Mills's Chapter 15, "The Higher Immorality," in *The*

114

Power Elite (paper ed.; New York: Oxford University Press, 1959).
15. See *How to Talk Dirty,* pp. 64-5; *Essential Lenny Bruce,* pp. 298-300; "Would You Sell Out Your Country?", *Lenny Bruce: To Is a Preposition, Come Is a Verb* (Douglas Records 2); "Communism," *Midnight Concert.*
16. See *How to Talk Dirty,* p. 74; *Essential Lenny Bruce,* pp. 15-34; "The Defiant Ones," *Lenny Bruce: "I Am Not a Nut, Elect Me!"* (Fantasy Records 7007); "How to Relax Your Colored Friends at Parties," *Lenny Bruce—American* (Fantasy Records 7011); "A White, White Woman and a Black, Black Woman," *To Is a Preposition.*
17. See, among others, *How to Talk Dirty,* pp. 43, 67-71, 155-56, 159-60, 179-81, 189-93; *Essential Lenny Bruce,* pp. 222-24, 227-40, 250-54, 256-62, 281-92, 296-98; "To Come," "The Perverse Act," "Tits and Ass," "A Pretty Bizarre Show," "Dirty Toilet," "Blah-Blah-Blah," *To Is a Preposition;* side 1, *Lenny Bruce Is Out Again* (Philles Records PHLP 4010); *Lenny Bruce: The Berkeley Concert* (Bizarre/Reprise Records 6329).
18. See *How to Talk Dirty,* pp. 23,65.
19. See ibid., pp. 68-9, 73-5, 90-91, 103-04, 120-23; *Essential Lenny Bruce,* pp. 57-69, 290-93; "Religions, Inc.," *Sick Humor;* "Christ and Moses," *Midnight Concert.*
20. "The Tribunal," *"I Am Not a Nut."*
21. *How to Talk Dirty,* pp.90-91; *Essential Lenny Bruce,* pp. 57-61; "Christ and Moses," *Midnight Concert.*
22. *How to Talk Dirty,* pp. 59, 64, 232; *Essential Lenny Bruce,* pp. 76-80, 92-94, 96, 160-64; "Ike, Sherm and Dick," *Sick Humor; Essential Lenny Bruce: Politics.*
23. *How to Talk Dirty,* pp. 57-62, 210-16; *Essential Lenny Bruce,* pp. 147-59; "Three Commercials," *Lenny Bruce—American; Lenny Bruce Is Out Again; The Berkeley Concert;* "Pot Will Be Legal," *Essential Lenny Bruce: Politics.*
24. *How to Talk Dirty,* pp. 62, 91-92, 210, 222; *Essential Lenny Bruce,* pp. 291-293; "Father Flotski's Triumph," *Lenny Bruce's Interviews of Our Times* (Fantasy Records 7001); "Father Flotski's Triumph" (unexpurgated), *Lenny Bruce—American.*
25. "If I do anything more than once, it's a bit." Lenny Bruce quoted by Paul Krassner on the liner notes to *The Midnight Concert.*
26. As revealed by "The Palladium," *"I Am Not a Nut";* cf. *Essential Lenny Bruce,* pp. 103-110.
27. "The Tribunal," *"I Am Not a Nut".*
28. *How to Talk Dirty,* p. 17.
29. "The Steve Allen Show," *"I Am Not a Nut".*
30. See, e.g., Wilhelm Reich, *The Mass Psychology of Fascism* (paper ed.; n.p.: The Albion Press, 1970). "Suppression of the natural sexuality in the child . . . makes the child apprehensive, shy, obedient, afraid of authority, 'good' and 'adjusted' in the authoritarian sense; it paralyzes the rebellious forces because any rebellion is laden with anxiety; it produces, by inhibiting [first] sexual curiosity and sexual thinking in the child, a *general* [emphasis added] inhibition

of thinking and of critical faculties. In brief, the goal of sexual suppression is that of producing an individual who is adjusted to the authoritarian order [of class society] and who will submit to it in spite of all misery and degradation. At first, the child has to adjust to the structure of the authoritarian miniature state, the family; this makes it capable of later subordination to the general authoritarian system . . ." (pp. 24-25). This sexual inhibition, "with the aid of religious fear," produces a "necessity for sexual self-control, for maintenance of sexual repression, [leading] to the development of compulsive, emotionally highly charged ideas of honor, duty, courage and self-control" (p. 46). It was precisely such "compulsive, emotionally charged ideas" that Bruce was at pains to counter in his satirizing of the conventional wisdom of, in his words, "the good-good culture." See *Essential Lenny Bruce,* pp. 222-67, 281-304, and passim.; "Would You Sell Out Your Country," *To Is a Preposition.* To judge by the incidents in his autobiography, Bruce himself had a lively sexual curiosity as a child, which was actively discouraged, to say the least, by his mother and especially his Orthodox Jewish Aunt Mema. The opening paragraph of the autobiography, for example, is an inventory of what Bruce called "erotic folklore," items of which "were related daily to my mother by Mrs. Janesky, a middle-aged widow who lived across the alley"—to wit: "Filipinos come quick; colored men are built abnormally large ('Their wangs look like a baby's arm with an apple in its fist'); ladies with short hair are Lesbians; if you want to keep your man, rub alum on your pussy." *How to Talk Dirty,* p. 1. See also Bruce's account of men allegedly exposing themselves to his mother and Aunt Mema, *The Berkeley Concert* and *Essential Lenny Bruce,* pp. 208-09.

31. "Dirty Toilet," *To Is a Preposition.*
32. For an account of Bruce's "obscenity" arrest and trial in San Francisco, in which numerous instructive excerpts from the trial transcript are included, see *How to Talk Dirty,* pp. 132-63; and also *Essential Lenny Bruce,* pp. 244-47, 254-56, 258-59.
33. "A Pretty Bizarre Show," *To Is a Preposition.*
34. "Blah-Blah-Blah," ibid.
35. Ibid.
36. *How to Talk Dirty,* pp. 132-33, 138-39; *Essential Lenny Bruce,* pp. 245-47; "Blah-Blah-Blah," *To Is a Preposition.*
37. "Blah-Blah-Blah," *To Is a Preposition.*
38. *How to Talk Dirty,* pp. 159-60; *Essential Lenny Bruce,* pp. 250-52; "To Come," *To Is a Preposition.*
39. "To Come," *To Is a Preposition.*
40. *Essential Lenny Bruce,* p. 252. I have altered the punctuation slightly, and also included some phrases from the same bit in *How to Talk Dirty,* p. 70.
41. "To Come," *To Is a Preposition.*
42. *Essential Lenny Bruce,* p. 253.
43. "To Come," *To Is a Preposition.*

44. *How to Talk Dirty,* p. 156; see also p. 68, and *Essential Lenny Bruce,* p. 287.
45. *How to Talk Dirty,* p. 181.
46. Ibid., p. 188.
47. Ibid., p. 193.
48. Ibid., and *Essential Lenny Bruce,* p. 283.
49. *How to Talk Dirty,* p. 192-93.
50. Ibid., p. 191.
51. Ibid., pp. 191-92; ellipses in original. Cf. *Essential Lenny Bruce,* pp. 234-35.
52. *Essential Lenny Bruce,* p. 147; see also pp. 147-59; *How to Talk Dirty,* pp. 57-62.
53. "Pot Will Be Legal," *Essential Lenny Bruce: Politics.*
54. See Mills, *Power Elite,* passim.
55. See Walter and Miriam Schneir, *Invitation to an Inquest* (Garden City, N.Y.: Doubleday, 1965); Staughton Lynd, "Lying in State: The Problem of Government Prevarication," *Monthly Review,* XVIII: 5 (October 1966), pp. 36-42.
56. *How to Talk Dirty,* p. 91; emphasis and last ellipsis in original.
57. See *Essential Lenny Bruce,* pp. 298-300.
58. "Would You Sell Out Your Country?", *To Is a Preposition.*
59. According to Dick Schaap, Afterword to *How to Talk Dirty,* pp. 237, 240. Bruce himself, however, states (in ibid., p. 2) that he was eight years old in 1932, which would have made his age 41 or 42 at his death in 1966.
60. "Communism," *Midnight Concert.*
61. See also *Essential Lenny Bruce,* pp. 160-63. Lenny further challenged liberal dogma of the early 1960s by his spirited defense of Fidel Castro and the Cuban Revolution from the standpoint of a poor Cuban *campesino;* and he also upheld the Castro government's demand to have the U.S. vacate its naval base at Guantanamo Bay and return the harbor there to the Cuban nation. His remarks on this subject can be found on record 1, side 1 of *Lenny Bruce: Carnegie Hall: February 4, 1961* (United Artists UAS 9800), a complete recording of the performance from which the earlier United Artists release, *The Midnight Concert,* was excerpted. Unfortunately, this later album was issued too late for discussion in the text.
62. "The Bomb and Political Bullshit," *Essential Lenny Bruce: Politics.*
63. Foreword to *How to Talk Dirty,* p. ix. Tynan adds: "Myself, I wished he had broadened his viewpoint by a little selective reading of Marx as well as Freud" (ibid.). Marx, in particular, might have helped Bruce attain a more accurate perspective on the judicial branch of government, especially inasmuch as he already had observed the corruption of the executive branch (discussed immediately below). Instances of Bruce's failure to comprehend the true nature of the legal-judicial system can be seen in *Essential Lenny Bruce,* pp. 267, 280.

64. *How to Talk Dirty,* p. 232; virtually the same remark occurs, without the reference to Sahl, in *Essential Lenny Bruce,* p. 76.

65. *Essential Lenny Bruce,* p. 76. Unfortunately, as indicated above in note 63, Bruce did have illusions regarding the judiciary.

66. Ibid., p. 77.

67. See *Essential Lenny Bruce,* pp. 160-64.

68. "The Bomb and Political Bullshit," *Essential Lenny Bruce: Politics.*

69. "Black Democracy and Liberals," ibid.

70. *Essential Lenny Bruce,* p. 79.

71. According to Leo Rosten, *The Joys of Yiddish* (New York: McGraw Hill, 1968), p. 299, *rachmones,* meaning pity, compassion, "lies at the heart of Jewish thought and feeling. All of Judaism's philosophy, ethics, hierarchy of values, are saturated with a sense of, and heightened sensitivity to, *rachmones.*" No one exemplified this better than Bruce, as I shall discuss in the following pages. See also: *Essential Lenny Bruce,* pp. 97-100; *The Berkeley Concert;* "Johnson," *Essential Lenny Bruce: Politics.*

72. *Lenny Bruce Is Out Again.*

73. *Essential Lenny Bruce,* p. 113.

74. This bit, as well as the preceding quote, is found in *Essential Lenny Bruce,* pp. 17-18.

75. "Black Democracy and Liberals," *Essential Lenny Bruce: Politics.*

76. Bruce had, in fact, at one time been employed as a movie scriptwriter, and was offered a similar job in television — but his numerous arrests by that time kept him from being "cleared" by the studio legal department. See *How to Talk Dirty,* pp. 120-23, 227-30.

77. *Essential Lenny Bruce,* pp. 28-31.

78. "The Defiant Ones," *"I Am Not a Nut."*

79. See *Essential Lenny Bruce,* pp. 20-26.

80. "How To Relax Your Colored Friends At Parties," *Lenny Bruce — American.*

81. *Essential Lenny Bruce,* p. 24 (slight alterations in punctuation).

82. See ibid., pp. 57-61.

83. Both quotes from *How to Talk Dirty,* p. 75; ellipsis in original.

84. "There are actually fourteen signs in the lobby of St. Patrick's Church on Fifth Avenue [in New York], all reading: 'Do Not Enter Unless Properly Dressed for Church.'" Paul Krassner, album notes to *The Midnight Concert.*

85. *Midnight Concert.*

86. As I argue for Malcolm in *Black Nationalism and the Revolution in Music,* pp. 64-67, 256.

87. The full title is *El Hajj Malik — The Dramatic Life and Death of Malcolm X.* See Clive Barnes's *New York Times* Service feature, "Fine Tribute to Malcolm X," *San Francisco Chronicle,* December 1, 1971, p. 50.

88. I was, as mentioned previously, a graduate student at the University of California at Berkeley during the early 1960s, and was

politically active in Slate, the left-liberal organization that was the immediate predecessor of the Free Speech Movement, as well as a shorter-
lived group, the Students for Racial Equality. It was the latter group,
whose role in campus politics I have never seen adequately analyzed,
that was the first student organization to raise the issue which ultimately precipitated the Free Speech Movement—namely, the right
of students to raise money on campus for the use of the Student Non-
violent Coordinating Committee in the South. (See, e.g., the *Daily
Californian* for May and June 1960, and *Black Nationalism and
the Revolution in Music,* p. 114.) In any event, my impression is
that Bruce's work was relatively well known and he himself was
admired in the political-cultural circles in which I traveled.
89. *Essential Lenny Bruce,* p. 308; *How to Talk Dirty,* p. 238.
90. Spector was a high school classmate of my younger brother;
his age at the time of Bruce's death would therefore have been in
the neighborhood of 26.
91. *Lenny Bruce Is Out Again.*
92. Quoted by Orrin Keepnews in "Without Apology! The Existential Jazz Aura of Lenny Bruce," *Down Beat,* November 3, 1966,
p. 42.
93. See *The Great Society with Grace Slick: Conspicuous Only in
Its Absence* (Columbia Records CS 9624). "Father Bruce" was composed by four members of the Great Society: Grace and Darby Slick,
Darby's brother Jerry, and rhythm guitarist David Minor (listed
on the album as "D. Minor"!).
94. *The Berkeley Concert.*
95. See Frank Kofsky, "Frank Zappa Interview," in *The Age of
Rock: Sounds of the American Cultural Revolution* (paper ed.; New
York: Vintage Books, 1969), ed. Jonathan Eisen, p. 259.
96. The figure of nineteen busts is given in *How to Talk Dirty,* p.
188.
97. See, e.g., the leaflet circulated "by a couple of 19-year-old college students" at Bruce's 1962 San Francisco "obscenity" trial, ibid.,
pp. 150-51.
98. *The Power Elite,* p. 334.
99. Quoted, with ellipsis, in *How to Talk Dirty,* p. 122.
100. Ibid., pp. 185-88.
101. See ibid., pp. 194-95; "The Irony of Lenny Bruce," *San Francisco Sunday Examiner and Chronicle,* October 31, 1971. "As one
of the New York assistant district attorneys remorsefully told Bruce's
lawyer, Martin Garbus: 'We drove him into poverty and bankruptcy
and then murdered him. We all knew what we were doing. We used
the law to kill him.'" *Newsweek,* as quoted by James Walsh, "A Stand-
Up Jewish Comic Who Wasn't Very Funny Because He Always Told
the Truth," *Gallery,* November 1972, p. 35; see also Martin Garbus,
Ready for the Defense (paper ed.; New York: Avon Books, 1971),
pp. 89-90. Garbus also reveals (pp. 95-96) that most of the younger
attorneys employed by the city refused to participate in the prosecution of Bruce when requested by District Attorney Frank Hogan.

One of these younger lawyers, Jerry Harris, later told Garbus that he was "glad" that he "had nothing to do with it. I saw and heard about Lenny during and after the trial. The case helped to kill and destroy him. It was terrible. . . . I'm glad I don't have Bruce on my conscience" (quoted, p. 144). Incidentally, the "conviction-prone" judge who presided over the trial, John M. Murtagh, more recently served the same prosecutorial function in the New York Panther 21 case (pp. 98, 125). Notwithstanding the best efforts of the Ho-gan-Murtagh team, the "obscenity" conviction was overturned — twice — at the appellate level (pp. 142-43). Bruce's vindication, however, came posthumously.

102. "The Irony of Lenny Bruce," *San Francisco Sunday Examiner and Chronicle,* October 31, 1971; *How to Talk Dirty,* p. 224.
103. *How to Talk Dirty,* pp. 210-216, 224-27; the quote appears on p. 211.
104. Ibid., p. 188.
105. Ibid., pp. 227-31.
106. Ibid., p. 230.
107. Quoted in ibid., p. 189; emphasis added.
108. Ibid.; emphasis and ellipsis in original.
109. *Essential Lenny Bruce,* p. 306.
110. See *How to Talk Dirty,* p. 231.
111. Apparently, Lenny suffered from chronic bouts with illnesses that he believed he had contracted during his period of enlistment in the navy in World War II. See ibid., pp. 167-71, 173-79, 211-16, 224-25.
112. *How to Talk Dirty,* p. 230; *Essential Lenny Bruce,* pp. 258-59.
113. As is also the case with Malcolm X.
114. See *Essential Lenny Bruce,* p. 149; *How to Talk Dirty,* p. 164.
115. "Pot Will Be Legal," *Essential Lenny Bruce: Politics.*
116. *How to Talk Dirty,* p. 230; emphasis in original.
117. See *Essential Lenny Bruce,* pp. 70-75.
118. *Lenny Bruce Is Out Again.*
119. *How to Talk Dirty,* p. 1.
120. *Essential Lenny Bruce,* p. 197. For more of Lenny's comments, direct and indirect, on the break-up of his marriage, see: *Essential Lenny Bruce,* 164-168, 197-205, passim; *How to Talk Dirty,* pp. 116-19; "Marriage, Divorce and Motels," *Lenny Bruce—American;* and various remarks on *The Midnight Concert* and *Lenny Bruce Is Out Again.*
121. See, e.g., *Essential Lenny Bruce,* pp. 101-10, 145-46; "White-Collar Drunks," "The Steve Allen Show," "The Tribunal," "The Palladium," *"I Am Not a Nut."*
122. Compare, for instance, "Communism," *Midnight Concert,* with "Capitalism Is Best," *Essential Lenny Bruce,* pp. 85-86.
123. E.g., the two versions of "Father Flotski's Triumph," on *Lenny Bruce's Interviews of Our Times* (Fantasy Records 7001) and, un-expurgated, on *Lenny Bruce—American.* Cf. *Essential Lenny Bruce,* pp. 179-83.

124. E.g., "Christian of the Year," "Frank Sinatra and Albert Maltz," "Five Minutes of Geography and Ten Minutes of Cocksucking," "Adolf Eichmann," *Essential Lenny Bruce,* pp. 291, 300-04; *How to Talk Dirty,* p. 182.

125. "Airplane Glue," *Lenny Bruce – American; Essential Lenny Bruce,* p. 155.

126. *How to Talk Dirty,* p. 17.

127. See ibid., pp. 132-63 passim.

128. See my *Black Nationalism and the Revolution in Music,* pp. 9-16, 40-42, 54-57, 149-50, and Chapter 1, "Critiquing the Critics." In what I believe to be his last interview, the late and incredibly gifted John Coltrane discussed the way in which his music was received by writers for *Down Beat,* the jazz magazine of largest circulation in the U.S.: "Oh, that was terrible. I couldn't believe it, you know, it just seemed so preposterous. It was so ridiculous, man, that's what bugs me. It was absolutely ridiculous, because they made it appear that we didn't even know the first thing about music — the first thing. And there we were, really trying to push things ahead." *Black Nationalism and the Revolution in Music,* p. 242; see also pp. 235-37 for other comments on this subject by Coltrane.

129. *How to Talk Dirty,* p. 6.

130. See, e.g., "Shelly Berman/Chicago/Night-Club Owners," *Lenny Bruce – American.*

131. Thus Bruce invoked "Jewish" and *"goyish"* (literal translation: non-Jewish, gentile) as polar antipodes to categorize the universe. Anything hip, tasteful, far out, or despised by the WASP culture was Jewish; anything icky, square, corny or otherwise lame was *goyish.* He therefore considered Count Basie, Ray Charles, Eugene O'Neill, Dylan Thomas, as well as himself and all Italians, to be Jewish. Instant potatoes, the Marine Corps ("heavy *goyim* [plural of *goy*], dangerous"), white bread, trailer parks ("so *goyish* that Jews won't go near them") and Steve Allen were among things *goyish.* See *Essential Lenny Bruce,* pp. 41-44 (quotes are from pp. 41-42), and *How to Talk Dirty,* pp. 6-7.

Lenny also intensely disliked the Great WASP Midwest (with the possible exception of Chicago); Milwaukee, for instance, was "like the Grey Line [tours] *en masse*" (p. 120). Small Midwestern towns, such as Lima, Ohio, were even worse: they were "disaster areas," pure and simple (p. 125). His comments on the ordeals of performing in Milwaukee and Lima are on pp. 119-31, and "Lima, Ohio," *Lenny Bruce – American.*

132. See the discussion of "Anglo-conformity" — a politer term for the truth I have put more baldly above — in Milton M. Gordon, *Assimilation in American Life: The Role of Race, Religion and National Origins* (paper ed.; New York: Oxford University Press, 1964), pp. 85-114 passim; and also, E. Digby Baltzell, *The Protestant Establishment: Aristocracy and Caste in America* (New York: Random House, 1964).

133. *Essential Lenny Bruce,* p. 42; minor changes in punctuation.

134. Ibid., p. 40 (again with minor alterations). I have here quoted the beginning of a longer bit; at the point I have broken off, the tone abruptly becomes lighter and funnier, as Bruce discusses the alleged Jewish killing of Christ: "Alright. I'll clear the air once and for all, and confess. Yes, we did it. I did it, my family. I found a note in my basement. It said: 'We killed him. Signed, Morty.'

"And a lot of people say to me, 'Why did you kill Christ?'

"'I dunno . . . it was one of those parties, got out of hand, you know.'

"We killed him because he didn't want to become a doctor, that's why we killed him" (pp. 40-41).

And elsewhere, "Now the Jews celebrate this holiday, *Rosh Hashonah* and *Yom Kippur,* where they, actually, they celebrate the killing of Christ. Underground. You know, when they all get loaded, and, you know, they just—

"'Oh, ho ho! We killed him! Ho, ho! More chicken soup! Oh, ho ho ho!'

"You know, kids running around with wooden sticks in the backyard: 'C'mon. Come up the hill! Come up the hill to Gethsemane!'

"You know" (pp. 36-37, with modifications of spelling and punctuation).

And so on. Bruce's sense of timing was so exquisite that he knew precisely how much serious discussion his audiences could (or would) absorb before the leavening of laughter was required. Hence no matter how serious the bit, he usually sought to bring it to its climax with a sudden twist of humor, more often than not of the bizarre variety. "Christ and Moses" is an excellent case in point. See *Essential Lenny Bruce,* pp. 35-36, 58-61; *The Midnight Concert.*

135. *Essential Lenny Bruce,* pp. 41-42; *How to Talk Dirty,* pp. 6-7; the quote is from p. 7.

136. *Essential Lenny Bruce,* pp. 38-39. On pp. 39-40, there is a brief vignette of a Jewish boy returning from military academy for a visit to his parents on New York's formerly very Jewish Lower East Side. Approaching the house, the boy mutters (in an Ivy League voice): "I don't wanna be there with those Mockies [derogatory slang term for Jews]! I don't wanna look at them anymore, with their onion-roll breaths. [On the page just previous, Bruce had described his Orthodox-Jewish Aunt Mema: "[T]he mole with hair in it, her breath always smelled from onion rolls, you know?"] I found something new at Fort Loeb, and a girl who doesn't know anything about the Lower East Side." See also *"Goyisha Punim* [Gentile Faces] vs. Jewish Chicks," p. 221.

137. See ibid., pp. 47-48; "Point of View," record 1, side 1, *Lenny Bruce: Carnegie Hall.* In the latter probing of his ambivalence, Bruce brings great semantic precision to bear in distinguishing between the phrases "glad I'm Jewish" and "proud to be Jewish." Only a masochist, according to him, could honestly claim to be "glad" about being Jewish.

138. *The Berkeley Concert.*

139. *The Power Elite,* pp. 335 ff.

140. Myron S. Kaufman, *Remember Me to God* (paper ed.; New York: Signet Books, 1958).

141. See the account of the Congress for Cultural Freedom by Christopher Lasch, "The Cultural Cold War: A Short History of the Congress for Cultural Freedom," Chapter 3 in *The Agony of the American Left* (paper ed.; New York: Vintage Books, 1969). Lasch does not say as much per se, but it is obvious that U.S.-born Jews, such as Melvin Lasky, Irving Kristol, Sol Stein, and Norman Jacobs, were disproportionately prominent in the founding of the CCF and its house organ, *Encounter* magazine.

142. See ibid., pp. 71-72, 85-90.

143. See my comments about the Jewish war criminal Walt Whitman Rostow, architect of Lyndon Johnson's "Plan No. 6" for the destruction from the air of Vietnamese society (and author of the greatly overrated tract on *The Stages of Economic Growth*), "Vietnam and Social Revolution," *Monthly Review,* XVIII:10 (March 1967), pp. 28-29.

144. Daniel Bell, *The End of Ideology* (paper ed.; New York: Collier Books, 1961) p. 311.

145. *Essential Lenny Bruce,* p. 221.

146. As he does in "The Palladium," *"I Am Not a Nut,"* and his "Hey, Masked Man!" fantasy, *Lenny Bruce Is Out Again,* to name only two.

147. See the picture on the third (unnumbered) page following p. 82, *How to Talk Dirty.*

148. See Lasch, *Agony of the American Left,* pp. 70-72; the quote is on p. 72. Lasch also points out (p. 71) that Fiedler attacked critics of McCarthy and McCarthyism.

149. Quoted in ibid., p. 87.

150. *How to Talk Dirty,* p. 91; ellipsis and second emphasis in original.

151. See *The Joys of Yiddish,* pp. 299-300. Not surprisingly, perhaps, Aaron Antonovsky found that *all* of a group of overwhelmingly middle-class (only seven workers, or 12 percent of the total, out of fifty-eight sampled), middle-aged (median age, 43) Jewish males felt that the Rosenbergs should be executed precisely because they had disgraced the "good" (i.e., nonradical) Jews such as themselves. At issue was not at all the abstract guilt or innocence of the Rosenbergs, but the consideration that the alleged activities of the couple might serve to inflame gentile opinion against Jews generally, thus interfering with their private ambitions to "get ahead." To avoid this eventuality, it seems, Jewish middle-class and professional people far outstripped their non-Jewish counterparts in rabidly baying for the Rosenbergs' death. See Antonovsky, "Like Everyone Else, Only More So: Identity, Anxiety, and the Jew," in Maurice R. Stein, Arthur J. Vidich, and David Manning White, eds., *Identity and Anxiety: Survival of the Person in Mass Society* (Glencoe, Ill.: The Free Press, 1960), pp. 428-34.

152. In 1968 *Commentary,* published by the American Jewish Committee, conducted a survey on the theme of "Jewishness and the Younger Intellectuals" among those of Lenny Bruce's age group

(roughly, early thirties to early forties). The results of this survey revealed, according to Milton Gordon, "an overwhelming estrangement from the ideologies, issues, and concerns of Jewish communal life in America." *Assimilation in American Life*, p. 231. Two other researchers, Sidney Goldstein and Calvin Goldscheider, have likewise observed that Reform Jewish congregations—that is, the most Protestantized and assimilated of the three Jewish denominations (Orthodox, Conservative and Reform)—have a disproportionately large number of the college- and post-college-educated as members, once more indicating the tendency of the Jewish educated classes to head the flight from Jewish tradition. See Goldstein and Goldscheider, *Jewish Americans: Three Generations in a Jewish Community* (paper ed.; Englewood Cliffs, N.J.: Prentice-Hall, 1968), pp. 183, 241.

153. For instance: "Certainly on an intellectual level I cannot buy the mysticism attached to any man-made religious object, whether it be the [Jewish] *mezuzah* nailed to the door sill . . . or the white plastic statues that Father Gregory from Louisiana has manufactured, the proceeds of which go to building segregated Catholic schools. . . ." *How to Talk Dirty*, p. 104.

154. "Christ and Moses," *The Midnight Concert; Essential Lenny Bruce*, p. 35.

155. *Essential Lenny Burce*, pp. 61, 65; "Religions, Inc.," *Sick Humor of Lenny Bruce.*

156. I have combined two variations of this bit: *How to Talk Dirty*, p. 184, and *Essential Lenny Bruce*, pp. 35-36. See also Myron Kaufman's essentially similar burlesque of a Reform *shule*—the rabbi even talks the same as Lenny's!—in *Remember Me to God.*

157. The paradigm assimilationist in this regard is Richard Amsterdam in Kaufman's *Remember Me to God.*

158. Leo Rosten, *The Joys of Yiddish*, p. 502. Rosten adds: "Beginning with Erza, Jewish scholars established the precept that no man should use the *Torah* [Jewish law] as a 'spade' with which to dig for wealth. The great names of the *Talmud* [interpretation of the law] are the names of workmen-scholars: Hillel was a wood-chopper; Shammai, a surveyor; Ishmael, a tanner; Abba Hoshaiah, a launderer" (ibid.). Compare this with Lenny's dictum: "I knew in my heart by pure logic that any man who calls himself a religious leader and owns more than one suit is a hustler as long as there is someone in the world who has no suit at all" (*How to Talk Dirty*, p. 75). Lenny's position was much closer to that of the rabbi of Jewish tradition than that of most contemporary rabbis.

159. Ibid., pp. 300-01; emphasis added.

160. Ibid., pp. 216-17; emphasis added.

161. Ibid., pp. 414-15; ellipsis in original.

162. *Essential Lenny Bruce*, p. 112. Besides his goodness, the outstanding characteristic of the *tzaddik* was his humility; see the first parable on *tzaddikim* in Rosten, *Joys of Yiddish*, p. 415. There is a better version of Lenny's *tzaddik* bit above that is unfortunately too long to quote; but see *How to Talk Dirty*, pp. 234-36. Lenny's

repeated insistence that he wanted to be neither a martyr nor a hero was, like his "Masked Man" scenario, a derivation from the tradition of the *tzaddik.*

163. But see Pauline Kael's insightful discussion of the Jewish contribution to another field of humor, musical comedy, in "The Current Cinema: A Bagel with a Bite Out of It," *The New Yorker,* November 13, 1971, pp. 133-39 passim.

164. It is tempting to speculate in this connection whether Lenny's attempt to earn his livelihood by masquerading as a priest at one point was not in part also an effort to come to terms with his own unfulfilled and perhaps unconscious desire to function and be recognized as a spiritual leader. See *How to Talk Dirty*, pp. 71-104; *Essential Lenny Bruce,* pp. 53-54. Lenny's admiration of Moses — the most important Jewish teacher (rabbi) — lends further support to this speculation. See, e. g., *How to Talk Dirty,* p. 73.

165. For an illustrative paradigm, see "Esther Costello Story," *"I Am Not a Nut."* Consider also the following example: "I sort of felt sorry for . . . flies. . . . Even though they were supposed to carry disease, I never heard anybody say he caught anything from a fly. My cousin gave two guys the clap, and nobody ever whacked *her* with a newspaper." *How to Talk Dirty,* p. 2.

166. *The Joys of Yiddish,* pp. xxiii-xxiv.

167. Thus definitions and derivations for most of these terms can be found in Harold Wentworth and Stuart B. Flexner, comps., *Dictionary of American Slang* (New York: Crowell, 1960), which was published more than a decade ago and clearly antedates the emergence of the counter-culture.

168. *How to Talk Dirty,* p. 156.

169. Orrin Keepnews, "Without Apology! The Existential Jazz Aura of Lenny Bruce," *Down Beat,* November 3, 1966, p. 42. Although suffering slightly from excess caution and a deficiency of empathy, this remains one of the *very* few secondary sources on Bruce that I found sufficiently valuable to cite. For a hilarious illustration of Keepnews' point about Bruce's ability to capture the spoken idiom of the Black musician *exactly,* see *Essential Lenny Bruce,* pp. 143-45; "The Interview," *Lenny Bruce's Interviews of Our Times;* and the complete version of this bit on "The Sound," *Lenny Bruce: "Thank You, Masked Man"* (Fantasy Records 7017).

170. *How to Talk Dirty,* p. 6.

171. *How to Talk Dirty,* pp. 116-19. It may be because he served such a lengthy and apparently not unpleasant apprenticeship in burlesque clubs that Lenny didn't have much use for the usual show-biz notions of what comprised a "good room." In "The Palladium," *"I Am Not a Nut,"* he illustrates the fallacious thinking of the typical nightclub comic obsessed with "good room" delusions. Lenny also sheds some incidental light on the nightclub situation in Southern California ("The pool's not in yet, but the patio's dry") in the same virtuoso performance.

172. The archetype here is Milton (Mezz) Mezzrow, who married

a Black woman, moved to Harlem and affected a Louis Armstrong speaking style for the rest of his life. See Mezzrow and Bernard Wolfe, *Really the Blues* (New York: Random House, 1948). I attempt to supply a theoretical explanation for this phenomenon of Black mentor/white disciple in the Introduction to *Black Nationalism and the Revolution in Music,* pp. 16-23.

173. I surmise that the "Joe" whom Lenny describes as "one of my best friends, a saxophone player," on p. 112 of *How to Talk Dirty,* is Maini; see also ibid., p. 96: "I got a new Kenny Drew album and Joe Maini is on it and he really sounds good." In his "Florence Zelk" (Lawrence Welk — the name was changed to avoid a libel suit) bit, Bruce tells us that the leader is looking for new musicians: "The whole rhythm section, Philly Joe Jones left him, Leroy Vinnegar, Miles [Davis]—they all split." Drummer Philly Joe Jones was to become one of Lenny's most devoted fans; see Keepnews, "Without Apology," *Down Beat,* November 3, 1966, pp. 20, 42; trumpeter Miles Davis was Philly Joe's employer throughout most of the 1950s. Bruce was in the habit of frequently saluting his friends by incorporating their names, usually at most improbable places, in his bits; he does this with Phil Spector, e. g., at the close of the second side of *Lenny Bruce Is Out Again,* a record Spector himself released.

174. *Essential Lenny Bruce,* p. 102; see also *How To Talk Dirty,* p. 197.

175. As an excellent case in point, hear the three versions of "My Favorite Things" recorded by John Coltrane over a period of several years: *My Favorite Things* (Atlantic Records SD 1361, 1960); *Selflessness* (Impulse Records AS-9161, 1963); *Live at the Village Vanguard Again* (Impulse Records AS-9124, 1966).

176. Keepnews, "Without Apology," *Down Beat,* November 3, 1966, pp. 21, 42. The bit quoted is in *Essential Lenny Bruce,* p. 92; see also *Sick Humor of Lenny Bruce.*

177. *How to Talk Dirty,* p. 46.

178. "I Just Do It and That's All," *To Is a Preposition.*

179. *Lenny Bruce—American.*

180. A variant of this bit is in *Essential Lenny Bruce,* pp. 194-95.

181. *Lenny Bruce Is Out Again.*

182. For Lenny's close ties to the world of Black musicians, see Keepnews, "Without Apology," *Down Beat,* November 3, 1966, pp. 20, 21, 42; *How to Talk Dirty,* pp. 46, 112, 119. In another article, Bruce discusses his ties to the jazz world, confirming in essence those hypotheses advanced above; see an interview by Ed Sherman, "George Crater [Sherman's literary pseudonym] Meets Lenny Bruce," in Gene Lees, ed., *Down Beat's Music 1960* (Chicago: Maher Publications, 1960), pp. 56-58. Bruce's spoof of Bela Lugosi movies, "Enchanting Transylvania," is on *Lenny Bruce's Interviews of Our Times,* and also *Essential Lenny Bruce,* pp. 172-76. Philly Joe Jones's *Blues for Dracula* has been out of print since the bankruptcy of Riverside Records, the company that originally issued it, in 1964.

Keepnews (p. 42) believes that a common interest in "obscure bad movies, the kind that seem to survive only in all-night fleabag theaters and on the triple-late shows of TV," helped cement Lenny's friendship with Philly Joe and other jazz musicians; and that this interest arose out of the dilemma of all performers with late-evening hours: "[T]he man [or woman] whose working day ends at 5 p.m. has plenty of places to stop for an unwinding cocktail, but what do you do when you quit work at 2 or 4 [the legal closing hour in New York City] in the morning?" I don't find Keepnews especially persuasive on either of these two points, however. To begin with, Lenny was linked to the fraternity of improvising musicians by a number of things, some of which I have sought to enumerate above, of greater significance than old horror films. Moreover, Lenny's career as a connoisseur of grade-B cinema began, by his own account, in childhood. Here, see *How to Talk Dirty*, p. 9.

183. "Without Apology," *Down Beat*, November 3, 1966, p. 42. This incident has a sorry sequel. Lenny was delighted at the chance to play before such a hip and congenial audience as the Jazz Workshop ordinarily drew. Moving to the Workshop, which is located on San Francisco's nightclub-dense Broadway, however, brought Lenny directly under the scrutiny of the district attorney's office and the police department. This, plus an entirely contrived and fraudulent arrest in Philadelphia a few days before (on a narcotics charge that was later thrown out of court), led to his undoing. Shortly after opening at the Workshop in October 1961, his use of the word "cocksucker" brought him a bust for obscenity — the first, but scarcely the last. Lenny was, of course, finally acquitted in San Francisco, and the charges in his Philadelphia arrest never got beyond the grand jury stage before being dismissed. It would therefore have seemed that Lenny had emerged unscathed and triumphant in his first two brushes with the supposed forces of "law and order." But his triumphs showed themselves to be more apparent than real, as hollow ultimately as his booking at the Jazz Workshop. The two arrests, coming in rapid succession, established Lenny's reputation with district attorneys and police as a man too dangerous to be allowed to roam loose, regardless of the fact that he was found innocent in both cases. As he explained it: "I guess what happens is, if you get arrested in Town A (Philadelphia) and then Town B (San Francisco) — with a lot of publicity — then when you get to Town C they *have* to arrest you or what kind of a shithouse town are *they* running?" (*How to Talk Dirty*, p. 180.)

With a bitter irony all too frequently found in Lenny's jagged career, what had looked at the outset like a rare opportunity to perform for his kind of people, musicians and their followers, turned out in retrospect to be the first link in a chain reaction that ended by sending Lenny to the grave.

184. Which comprises one of the central themes of my *Black Nationalism and the Revolution in Music;* see in particular the Introduction and chapters 1-7, 11, 12.

185. *Essential Lenny Bruce,* pp. 179-83; *Lenny Bruce's Interviews of Our Times; Lenny Bruce — American.*

186. *Sick Humor* and *Midnight Concert,* respectively.

187. *"I Am Not A Nut."*

188. "Communism," *The Midnight Concert;* "Black Democracy and Liberals," *Essential Lenny Bruce: Politics.* The relevant portions of these two bits do not appear in *Essential Lenny Bruce.*

189. *Essential Lenny Bruce,* p. 113.

190. "Black Democracy and Liberals," *Essential Lenny Bruce: Politics.* A mis-transcribed version of this excerpt, in which the words "at the Negro" are erroneously given as "to the Negro," appears in *Essential Lenny Bruce,* p. 16. Following Hollywood, Lenny usually typecast Pat O'Brien as the priest; hence, by extension, any authority figure.

191. See *How to Talk Dirty,* pp. 62, 91, 210, 222; *Essential Lenny Bruce,* pp. 291-93.

192. *Lenny Bruce's Interviews of Our Times; Lenny Bruce — American.*

193. Ibid.

194. Keepnews, "Without Apology," *Down Beat,* November 3, 1966, p. 42. I have made some very minor modifications in Keepnews' comments (e. g., introducing a third "ya-ta"); I have also prepared my own version of "Father Flotski's Triumph" by combining different portions from the two recorded variations, *Lenny Bruce's Interviews of Our Times* and *Lenny Bruce — American.* For yet a different version, see *Essential Lenny Bruce,* pp. 179-83.

195. *Lenny Bruce's Interviews of Our Times; Lenny Bruce — American.*